Middle Management
Survival Guide

Kevin McMahon

iUniverse, Inc.
New York Bloomington

Middle Management Survival Guide

iUniverse books may be ordered through booksellers or by contacting:

iUniverse
1663 Liberty Drive
Bloomington, IN 47403
www.iuniverse.com
1-800-Authors (1-800-288-4677)

ISBN: 978-0-595-52934-6 (pbk)
ISBN: 978-0-595-62986-2 (ebk)

Printed in the United States of America

Dedication

Three men have greatly influenced my life as a middle manager. The first was my first and only mentor, Bill Littlejohn. The second one is my father Robert L. McMahon. The final one is the owner of the company I currently work for, Brian Colleran.

Bill Littlejohn was my first boss as a young management trainee for a large nursing home in Durham, North Carolina. He was a large boned, tassel shoed, sharp dressing, Carolina drawling gentleman in his mid fifties. I was a transported Yankee from Ohio trying to get on top of the cultural differences between the Midwest and the Piedmont area of North Carolina all the while trying to learn what it was to be a manager.

Bill took me into his life and the unique culture of his facility where I was training to get my license as a nursing home administrator. He welcomed my newlywed wife and me into his family. He infected me with a terminal case of Carolina basketball fever. He also doled out helping measures of knowledge about the art of management as well as his own unique folksy, countrified wisdom. He gave freely of all the knowledge that he had accumulated throughout his hard knock career as a restaurant manager and nursing home administrator. He taught me that numbers were an exact science and that I should focus my management efforts on addressing only the things that were controllable in the world of business. He was a man of incomparable dignity and grace.

This book is also dedicated to my father, Robert L. McMahon. Like most men of his generation there was a rigid line dividing the world of work and the world of family. Aside from occasional Saturday morning trips to his office to scavenge office supplies (binder clips and mechanical pencils with

Republic Steel inscribed on them) while he caught up on work, I was largely ignorant of what my father did for a living.

Unfortunately (and fortunately) my first and final hint of what my father was all about in the world of work occurred at his retirement dinner. Unlike today's world my dad's employer gave him (and others) a grand going away dinner. There were probably hundreds of well-wishers in attendance.

Bob McMahon was a production planner for a now defunct steel company located in Northeast Ohio. He ran his department, which was responsible for planning production at a large hot roll bar mill that operated 24/7.

At the dinner person after person came to the dais to speak poignantly and pointedly about the kind of man and manager Bob was. There was humor and lightness and genuine affection expressed by all who spoke.

There was also a theme that ran through many of the comments. The theme was a characterization of Bob as a selfless man and manager. As I learned Bob was a manager who routinely built up the people who worked for him. He dispensed credit where it was merited and took the heat for problems that were the fault of no one. To all who worked for him he had succeeded in creating a positive work environment.

From that moment forward I committed myself to be the man and the manager that my father was. He allowed my career to merge with his in terms of values and commitment to the people side of the management equation. He made me a better man and manager by force of his example.

Finally this book is dedicated to Brian Colleran. Brian is an entrepreneur in the purest sense of the word. He went from a number crunching staff accountant to the owner and operator of a multi million-dollar company in the span of five years. Through his ascendancy into the world of wealth and power he has never lost his sense of where he came from and his belief in the ability of the people in his company to do a good job.

He once told me that he remembered what it was like to work for a man who was fixated on the negative. This boss would always beat him up for the three things he did not do well versus applauding the thirty-three things he was doing well. Brian resolved to a build a company that would accentuate the thirty- three things that are right and quietly support every manager in overcoming the three things that were not up to snuff. His approach to doing this was hands off and from a purposefully macro management distance.

Working for his company has been a breath of fresh air for me and every other manager who has had the good fortune of working for this man.

Brian doesn't call it Intuitment, (the approach to management introduced in this book) but that is what the nursing home managers in his company do on a daily basis. They use it as they confront unparalleled difficulties in delivering care and services to a very fragile and vulnerable segment of our population all the while having their every move scrutinized by suspicious and litigious customers, regulators and employees.

Brian allowed me to think and to breathe and to be the type of a manager who could create and take risks and exercise the full breadth of activities that make management fulfilling and at times down right exhilarating.

These three men have never heard of Intuitment. However, their subtle yet compelling influence on my development as a manager has opened my eyes to the existence and power imbedded in the use of this approach to management. This is an approach whose goal is to help managers survive and ultimately succeed. Success measured not in rungs on the corporate ladder but in a transformational worldview that restores a sense of sanity and balance to the world of middle managers.

Foreword

I have struggled to scratch out a livelihood as a middle manager working as a licensed nursing home administrator for the past twenty plus years. I have suffered under the tutelage of coldhearted orbs of all sorts. I am certain that collectively these taskmasters have carved years off of my lifespan. Through hard work, good fortune and God's grace I have been delivered from the majority of the travails that so characterize the life and times of a middle manager.

This book is something that has been jammed up inside of me for years and years. It arose from the desperation that was my life in the trenches of middle management. It is a testament to many who have worked above and beside me throughout my career. It is borne of the taskmaster and the tutor as well as the kindred souls that I have struggled with through trying times and circumstances.

I paint a rather bleak picture of the world faced by middle managers. I do this because I think it is a reality for many middle managers that do battle on the mean streets of corporate America in the decade of the ones. I also provide a way to approach management that I think will provide relief and success in many instances for many middle managers.

In addition to what shall follow let me say that I think it is critical for all of those who call themselves middle managers to have a "Plan B". I thought that "Plan B" was a universal code phrase for escape plan until a person I work with looked at me quizzically when I asked her what her "Plan B" was.

A "Plan B" is something, really anything of substance, which gives the middle manager a way to escape (hoped for, dreamt about or actual escape) the mind numbing tedium and/or gut choking anxiety that too often characterizes the life of a middle manager.

"Plan B's" can be tailored to allow a middle manager to better themselves in their career through education or training. "Plan B's" can be efforts to allow the middle manager to have a dream or the glimmer of a dream that will transport them from the battlefield that they visit on a daily basis. "Plan B's" can be hobbies or family activities that allow the middle manager to see that there is something more to life than the work-a-day world.

I was talking to a fellow dreamer/inventor and he mentioned that the two patents he has filed are languishing due to the fact that his day job is way too comfortable for him. He is an IT consultant with a variety of compliant/appreciative customers. His work is stimulating and filled with the black (working) and white (not working) of tech stuff. Because his work life is comfortable, his Plan B languishes.

By point of contrast middle management is an occupation that does not usually breed the same sort of complacency. The gut choking grayness that is the life of most middle managers makes the need to have, and regularly nourish, a Plan B an absolute imperative.

This book and a bunch of wild dreams constitute my "Plan B's". My logic always went that if my one "Plan B" does not work out my other "Plan B's" just might. Over the course of twenty years my "Plan B's" never delivered me from the harsh cold reality of my life as a middle manager. They did not change the difficulties inherent in placating the multiple publics that demand that their mutually exclusive goals be satisfied immediately and forever more. My dreams did not alter the harsh realities of a dysfunctional and diminished work force or short term driven, unyielding bosses.

However, my "Plan B's" did allow me to face the specter of a largely thankless job with a spark of courage and optimism that was not very often warranted by the circumstances on the ground in front of me. My "Plan B's" gave me hope that my tomorrows might be different from my yesterdays.

If you are a middle manager, always have at least one "Plan B". Keep it alive as you daily battle the forces arrayed against you.

Author's Note: The situations described in this book are purely fictional. Any similarities between these accounts and real people, places or situations is purely coincidental.

Contents

Chapter One

In The Beginning

My life as a middle manager has been an adventure to say the least. It is a journey that had a very fuzzy beginning twenty some years ago in a nursing home by the name of Hillhaven Rose Manor located in sleepy Durham, North Carolina. Since that beginning my career has followed a meandering course. I have held a variety of positions always in the field of long-term care administration, nursing homes and the like and always as a middle manager.

With an undergraduate degree in Psychology and a burning desire to save the world from itself, I am not certain how I ever came to enter the enchanted land of middle management. However, it is abundantly clear that twenty years into my journey I have become a virtual prisoner to the world of middle management.

During this imprisonment I have become utterly convinced and convicted of the fact that the most thankless job in all of the world falls to the person who gets the word manager (or a reasonable facsimile) printed somewhere on their name tag. This designation sentences the one so labeled to a life searching for answers and absolutes in a world filled with questions and ambiguity.

In addition to the daily frustrations that accompany mucking around in the murky grayness of organizations most middle manager's employment status from day to day is tenuous at best.

The middle manager is truly an employee who serves at the whim of those above him or her in the corporate hierarchy. Having personally experienced the ignominy of being pushed toward the cliff of involuntary termination I can attest to the fragility of the ties that bind manager to organization. A middle manager is in many ways the most expendable person in the organization and can be terminated as easily as a Yankee's manager with a penchant for missing the Fall Classic.

During a recent stint of unemployment that lasted for a period of months I was able to reflect mightily on the vaporous nature of life as a middle manager. The reasons for a manager's life being so tenuous are many and varied. Many of these dynamics are not subject to change.

However, the very dynamics of the management equation can be massaged to allow the middle manager to function at an optimal level. In addition, middle managers can change their worldview to allow themselves the maximum opportunity to survive as managers or at the very least preserve their dignity and sense of self worth.

This approach to management for the middle manager I have called Intuitment.

A Case Study

Intuitment is not a term that resides in the nomenclature of the business world at the present time. Intuitment is a new concept to the enterprise of managing people and organizations.

Possibly the best way to introduce Intuitment to the reader of this book is through an anecdotal account from the life and times of the penultimate middle manager, Eddie Travail.

Eddie Travail held the title of nursing home administrator. For all intents and purposes he was a middle manager. He had been a middle manager his entire working life.

In his position as a middle manager Eddie was caught in the no man's land between two very potent forces. Arrayed on the one side was an unrelenting organization composed of demanding, cynical, and unyielding employees and bosses. On the other side was an equally demanding, suspicious and litigious group of customers, regulators and consumer advocates. Eddie was caught square in this demilitarized zone between his organization and the external world, the workspace occupied by those who call themselves middle managers.

This anecdote, which is one of several sprinkled throughout this book, focuses on how Eddie responded to a situation that involved the reaction of his boss to a totally unexpected and unavoidable occurrence.

Eddie's boss was a man by the name of Mr. Bane (his given name was Jackson, his "friends" called him Jack). From his very first day under the tutelage of Mr. Bane, Eddie had learned that Mr. Bane's first name was MISTER. It was a lesson he would not soon forget as he learned the true nature of Mr. Bane's autocratic, manipulative, and bullying style of management.

Mr. Bane was an imposing presence. Eddie likened him physically and facially to Donald Trump. Additionally he had "The Donald's" temperament and approach to running an enterprise.

Eddie had learned through trial and error that the only thing worse than incurring Mr. Banes wrath for a screw up (Eddie's or anyone else's for that matter) was a failure to fully apprise him of all that was happening at the retirement facility they worked for by the name of Golden Rule Village.

It was at one such update session that the conversation turned to the weather that was in full January bloom. An unprecedented amount of snow had fallen and was accumulating rapidly.

"So Eddie, do we have any problems with the snow and ice building up on the roofs of our buildings?" Mr. Bane asked, innocently enough.

"Well, Mr. Bane, "Eddie stammered. "Now that you mention it we are seeing some leaks in the ceiling back in the kitchen area."

Mr. Bane glared across the table at Eddie with utter contempt and disbelief.

"Travail, how could you have allowed this to happen? Why haven't you addressed this situation all along? It didn't just start snowing yesterday, you know? Must I do all of the proactive thinking around here? Didn't we talk about this last week?"

"Yes sir, we did," Eddie lied.

"Well then Edddeee," Mr. Bane said in his exaggerated way whenever a meeting or conversation was over. "I suggest you get back to the kitchen and see to it that something is done to aggrandize this situation immediately (if "mister" was Mr. Bane's first name, then malapropism must have been his middle name).

When Eddie arrived in the service corridor he was greeted by the sight of his Maintenance Supervisor, Clayton Royce, standing on a ladder with his head and shoulders above the acoustical tile of the suspended ceiling.

"Well Clayton, what does it look like up there?" Eddie asked as he grabbed onto of the ladder and tried to peer up into the darkness.

Clayton Royce was the longest tenured supervisor at Golden Rule. He was plodding toward his sixty- fifth birthday and the promise of a carefree retirement. Eddie was always amazed that Clayton had been able to work for Mister Bane for the past fifteen years.

"Eddie, it does not look very good. It seems as though the leaks are moving in a straight line toward the main dining room."

"Well lets go outside and take a look at the roof," Eddie said, as he pulled on his coat and made his way to the loading dock door.

They were greeted by blinding sunlight that was exposing concrete for the first time in several months. As they stepped back from the building their eyes took in the full enormity of the snowfall. Easily two feet of snow covered the entire roof area with drifts of up to three feet in some areas.

Both men shook their heads in amazement as Billy Phelps joined them. Billy was a fixture in the kitchen at Golden Rule. The speculation always ran to the fact that Billy was homeless or bi-polar or both.

"So, gentlemen," Billy billowed as he blew air on his hands and followed their eyes to the thirty degree pitched, single story roof. "If I had to guess I would say that you must be wondering how to get that snow off of the roof before your fancy dining room becomes a glorified shower stall."

"Speaking of showers, Billy," Clayton said, as he pinched his nose and cast a disdainful look his way.

"Clayton," Eddie interjected, cutting short the sure to follow snipe session. "What do you think about the snow up there?"

"Boss, I'd say that if we have one more sunny day like today we will be looking at an insurance claim at this same time tomorrow."

Eddie knew that with the insurance claim a two month long stream of invective and recriminations from Mr. Bane would be sure to follow. Eddie knew that it was a scenario he could not allow to happen. The futility of the situation caused Eddie to close his eyes as he inclined his head toward the bright blue, winter sky.

Billy Phelps still looking on spoke up, "If this here were my roof, I'd think about getting a snow blower up there to clean it off."

There was a long silence among the three men.

"Clayton," Eddie began, turning to face his Maintenance Supervisor. "I really don't see that we have much choice. I will grant you that it sounds just a little crazy, but I really can't think of a better idea. Can you?"

Clayton's silence was all the answer Eddie needed. He asked Clayton to go to the shop to get his supply of ¼ inch yellow safety rope and the facility snow blower.

"Clayton, I'll meet you on the roof." Eddie said, as he briskly walked back into the building.

A ten-foot by ten-foot parapet sat atop the roof peak directly over the kitchen and dining room. The parapet held the exhaust and HVAC equipment for the kitchen and was surrounded by a three-foot wall. The parapet was accessible by a ladder that ran from a utility closet in the kitchen up to the roof.

As Eddie stood looking out over the three-foot wall, he could hear Clayton join him on the roof and begin to immediately tie the two lengths of rope off onto the mounting rings for the ductwork.

As Clayton began to loop the rope around his waist, Eddie stopped him short.

"Clayton what do you think you are doing?"

"Boss, I intend to put my best Scout Master skills to use and get this snow off of our roof. "

"Clayton, I can't let you do that. Take the rope off. I'll be the poor fool going out there. You have not gotten to within 300 days of retirement to fall and break your neck."

"Well, you are the boss, Boss," a relieved Clayton said, as he quickly untied the rope from his waist.

Eddie proceeded to tie the rope around his own waist and gingerly climb over the parapet wall and onto the snow and ice covered roof. With the other length of rope, Eddie pulled the snow blower onto the roof from the parking lot some twenty-feet below. He started blowing the snow off of the roof slowly at first. Soon, however, Eddie had a system and began to move the snow quite efficiently to the parking lot below.

As Eddie worked a group of gawking, dumbfounded employees began to gather. Within a matter of hours, Eddie had moved enough of the snow to allow the sun's warming rays to do the rest.

Several days later at the weekly Department Director meeting, Eddie was happy to report that the snow on the roof had not done any damage to the dining room.

Mr. Bane would never know the particulars of how the crisis was averted. The story, however, would be retold frequently over the coming weeks and months around the time clock and in the smoke room at Golden Rule Village.

Post Game Analysis

Whether he knew it or not, Eddie Travail had used Intuitment in dealing with this somewhat typical situation faced by middle managers. As middle management situations go it had all of the essential ingredients; a fire breathing boss, a time critical element, a workforce without a clear direction or answer, and finally a situation that would not be found in a mountain of policy and procedure manuals, college text books, or compendiums of laws and regulations.

Eddie was faced with a situation that required him to act. It was unlike anything he had faced in all of his life and work years. Yet Eddie's approach to dealing with this situation spoke volumes about the kind of manager Eddie had become and possibly more importantly the kind of person Eddie was.

Overarching Strategies, Attitudes and Values

Eddie had learned the value of doing jobs that no one wanted to do relatively early in his life. From scraping dishes in the college cafeteria to cleaning up after a resident who had a bowel accident in the dining room, Eddie believed that action was as important as managing. In some instances where the job was particularly onerous or difficult such as blowing snow off of a roof, getting things done was more important than managing.

Another overarching value that came into play in this little scene was the value encapsulated in the Golden Rule; "Do unto others, as you would have them do unto you."

Eddie was quite introspective when it came to how long he would have to work and what he would be doing on the eve of his retirement. He well imagined that he would be pushing large carts filled with supplies across the parking lot in the face of a stiff winter wind. He would be doing this because someone or another had called off from the kitchen and the only other person available to do this would be a 6-month pregnant dietary worker.

Needless to say Eddie had developed a soft spot in his heart for those closing in on retirement. Eddie's Maintenance Supervisor had his retirement within reach. Eddie knew that if he was six months away from his retirement, the last thing he would want to do is sustain a broken hip falling from a roof. Eddie went out on the roof with the snow blower instead of Clayton because he hoped that someday, someone would do the same for him when he was in Clayton's shoes.

Finally, Eddie was a humble man. Upon conquering the "snow on the roof dilemma" he did not do a happy dance, high five his Maintenance Supervisor, or run around congratulating himself and extolling his strengths as a manager. His reward was his ability to solve an interesting/unique problem. In so doing Eddie paved the way for his return to work tomorrow to fight yet another day.

Situation Analysis

Eddie was faced with a situation that required an immediate response on his part. Eddie was able to take in the situation and immediately discern the following:

- The snow would melt causing water damage to the ornate dining room in very quick order.

- Jack Bane had zero tolerance for problems. When Eddie heard the catch phrase, "failure to act proactively", Eddie knew that recriminations and disciplinary actions would fly fast and furious if any water damage occurred.

- Eddie had no idea what he could do to deal with the imminent disaster about to damage the finely sculptured ceilings. However, Eddie in analyzing the situation had the presence of mind to solicit ideas from other people.

In summary, Eddie's analysis of this situation was aimed at assessing the nature of the problem, understanding the Jack Bane dynamics that would ultimately judge the success or failure of his actions, and valuing and seeking the ideas of others.

Situation Response

Eddie's response to what ended up being a most unique set of circumstances illustrates three keys to effectively respond to a situation.

First Eddie responded to the situation. In light of the freakish nature of the occurrence, Eddie could have quite easily categorized it as an act of God and therefore beyond his ability to respond. He could have climbed underneath his desk and not come out until the arrival of Spring had rendered the problem moot. Instead Eddie Travail got out of his chair and left his office and inserted himself into the middle of the situation. He realized that he had to respond even though he had no idea at that point what he could do about the situation.

Secondly Eddie responded with a speed that the circumstances dictated. He knew that if the roof leaks extended beyond the kitchen and into the private dining room, employees would have new body cavities carved by Mr. Bane. In addition Eddie knew that people could very well loose their job over this.

Even though Eddie actively and happily fantasized about gaining his freedom from Mr. Bane via termination, the more likely outcome would be the expectation of Mr. Bane that Eddie would be forced to take decisive action (discipline/termination) against the employees in the Maintenance Department. With this as backdrop, acting too quickly was not a possibility in light of the situation and the down-the-road repercussions.

Finally, Eddie avoided the all too comfortable option of sending a surrogate to deal with the situation. When managers are confronted with messy situations that go well beyond the garden variety of grayness of most everything they confront the temptation to send a surrogate or intermediary can be overwhelming.

It was cold, the situation on the surface appeared hopeless and no one would have blamed Eddie if had simply called his Maintenance Director into his office and directed him to fix the problem himself. Eddie, however, sensed that he needed to be in the thick of the situation, on the scene divining an answer and direction to what appeared to be an unsolvable situation.

The Three Pillars – Not

In the early days of Eddie's career he would have faced the snow on the roof situation only with the three traditional tools available to middle managers; his management educational preparation, organizational policies and procedures, and laws/regulations.

Inevitably these traditional tools would have failed to generate a solution to the problem that Eddie was facing on that bitterly cold January day. No number of management texts, black plastic binders filled with policies and procedures, or volumes of federal code would have produced even an inkling as to what to do first.

Eddie may not have had a name for it but he had made use of Intuitment in solving a very unique problem and in the process saving himself and a whole bunch of other employees piles of grief.

Intuitment was instrumental to the survival of Edie Travail as well as the author of this book. Without a way to work outside of the confines of the traditional tools available to middle managers I would not have survived twenty some years as a middle manager. My survival was Eddie's survival. Our survival will hopefully form the basis for your survival as a middle manager.

The lot of a middle manager compares quite closely to the destiny of major league managers and coaches. The only difference (besides the compensation disparity) is that the comings and goings of middle managers are not publicized. Middle managers come and go in the relative obscurity of our corporate world.

This book is intended to aid the middle manager in their struggle to understand the grayness of the corporate battlefield, to recognize the abject paucity of the traditional tools available to them and finally to provide new and different tools and weapons with which to wage this war.

The end result will be an improvement in the survival rate for middle managers. This may very well translate into managers functioning at a higher level and increasing their longevity with their employer. However at the very least the psychic survival rate will be enhanced greatly by putting Intuitment into practice. Managers will understand the inherent difficulties of the manager's role and as a result view themselves and their performance in more objective/reality based terms.

Chapter Two

Mr. Roger's Neighborhood - NOT

Intuitment is a management tool intended for the middle managers of the world in their daily battle to survive. It is a tool that will ultimately improve the survivability of the insidiously dangerous game that they engage in on a daily basis

Middle managers carry out their responsibilities in the demilitarized zone of human commerce. They find themselves in a murky, gray swamp, square in the middle of the established forces of the business world. The forces that middle managers routinely grapple with are: upper management, the workforce, and customers or consumers.

The middle manager's job is to balance the conflicting priorities and needs of these three very disparate and potent forces. Not an easy task when individually and collectively these forces can have a great impact on the success or failure of a manager. This challenge is further complicated because the needs and demands of these groups can often times be in conflict with one another. At times the needs and demands can even be mutually exclusive.

THE BIG THREE

CUSTOMERS/CONSUMERS

Consumers (typically associated with products) and customers (typically associated with services) are driven by two basic self-interests.

Since this is a book for middle managers it will be written with heavy emphasis on, and orientation toward, customers. Since customers come in close

personal contact with middle managers and regularly interact with them it would seem logical to focus on them rather than consumers. In addition, customers are the ones who are close enough to get their fingers around the neck of the Eddie Travail's of the world and therefore are deserving of special attention.

Customers are ultimately driven to obtain the best price for the service/ product that they are purchasing. The drive to get the best bargain is firmly ingrained in our consumer driven culture. One need go no further than priceline.com to understand the buying public's obsession with getting the lowest possible price. The other major interest of customers is the desire to purchase the greatest quality possible. Quality is something that end-users pursue with a great vigor. In an optimal situation for an end user the greatest quality is secured at the lowest possible price. At this harmonic convergence of price and quality, users are happy and satisfied.

EMPLOYEES

Employees are motivated by a whole host of factors. Over the course of my career I have heard about/read about a slew of extrinsic and intrinsic factors that lead to job satisfaction for employees. Inevitably employee happiness boils down to satisfaction with pay and satisfaction with the job. These are elusive concepts as they vary greatly between employees as well as by day-of-the-week, stage-of-the-moon, etc. Suffice it to say that a well-paid employee doing a job that they find rewarding is a prescription for a productive, contributing member of the workforce.

BOSSES/UPPER MANAGEMENT

Many things motivate bosses. However, in the final analysis they are primarily concerned with the bottom line. A less than adequate bottom line renders all things secondary for the one who inhabits the offices in upper management row. The bottom line is driven by an abundance of factors but ultimately relies upon the ability to generate sufficient revenues while holding expenses in line, maximizing the former while minimizing the latter.

MONKEY, errr, MANAGER IN THE MIDDLE

You could very easily replace the word monkey with the term middle manager. The manager in the middle is a scene similar to the one where the short, slow footed eight year old is trying to get his baseball hat back from a group of three, taller bullies in the school playground. Like the monkey in the middle, the manager in the middle is faced with the unenviable task of trying to deal with forces that are bigger, numerically superior and ultimately in total control of the situation that he/she is charged with "controlling".

We will begin by examining the main points of conflict with the "Big Three" that consume the majority of a manager's resources (time, energy and emotion).

EMPLOYEES VS. BOSSES

This is the most traditional conflict that Middle Managers find themselves mediating. Bosses will talk a lot about job satisfaction and employee well being but the base motivation that they operate under is one of profit and bottom line success. Employees on the other hand will talk about being fulfilled at work but they are driven in the final analysis by the need to earn a life-sustaining wage for their labor.

These two groups (bosses and employees) are in the end working at cross-purposes to one another in terms of the universal currency of money. The profits of a company are an employee's foregone wage. The wages paid to employees are potentially lost profits for the company. These two groups carry on this battle for the goods and service's dollar in a contest refereed by the middle manager. The middle manager must try to pacify and at the same time represent these two groups to each other, attempting to satisfy the profit motives of the bosses while at the same time attempting to meet the wage needs and wants of employees. This can be a daunting task on a good day, in a company flush with money and low wage expectation employees (Has this ever happened in the history of the business world?).

BOSSES VS. CUSTOMERS

There have been many platitudes that have been cast down from the towers of corporate management that affirm the necessity of meeting the quality demands of the customer. When these high-minded words and goals are stripped away, there remains a basic conflict between the profit motive of bosses and the best-quality/lowest price motivation of customers.

As with the prior example, the goal of maximizing profits on the part of upper management is in direct conflict with the goal of the customer in minimizing the price for the product/service. The middle manager is often placed in the position of attempting to arbitrate this tug of war between these two groups. Whenever a price increase is passed down from on high, the middle manager is faced with the task of convincing the customer that the increase is justified. Alternatively the manager is charged with recouping market share that may disappear because the product or service is no longer price competitive.

Similarly, the middle manager is faced with the challenge of dealing with the disconnect between the customer and the bosses on the issue of quality. If there is a perception on either the part of the bosses, or the customers, that the quality of the good or service is lacking, the middle manager must not only explain but also take steps to correct the situation all the while attempting to balance any solution with the cost and resulting impact on prices and profits.

EMPLOYEES VS. CUSTOMERS

Typically in the service industry, employees come in daily and direct contact with the customers who are consuming the service being provided. This intimate contact establishes an environment that is ripe for conflict between these two parties.

The potential for conflict arises from the immediacy of the service for dollars transaction. The customer can reach out and touch the person who is responsible for the service that they are receiving and paying for. Alternatively the employee or provider of the service can feel the full force of dissatisfaction or happiness with what has been received.

The middle manager is oftentimes in the position of mediating these encounters. Whenever a customer has a problem with the service provided the middle manager must step into the breach and correct the situation to the satisfaction of the customer. Likewise, the middle manager must work with employees to help them deal with abusive, prejudicial, ignorant, or just plain ugly (a Southern expression that means ill tempered) customers.

The three situations outlined above pretty well represent the forces that fill the dynamic environment middle managers operate in, on a daily basis. These forces are aligned in direct opposition to one another. The middle manager occupies the demilitarized zone where conflicts between the big three are mediated in big and small ways. In a perfect world this would be a very doable task. Unfortunately ours is far from a perfect world.

LIFE IN THE "ONES"

The decade of that began with the arrival of Y2K I shall refer to as the ones. It may sound a bit absurd but I needed some way to refer to the current decade in shorthand fashion. My logic went something like this. We will call the decade beginning in 2010 as the "tens". Building on the way we name decimal places ones, tens, hundreds, why not call the decade of single digits the ones.

But I digress. Building on the pattern established during the last part of the twentieth century, the ones will be a time period of poisoned dynamics infecting all segments of society. In the business world this poison has been and will continue to be clearly in evidence. It is almost as if in the business world these dysfunctional dynamics are viewed as normal and acceptable because all things are fair in love, war and in the world of business.

Just because all things are fair doesn't mean they are not the ultimate bane of middle managers. The environment that business is transacted in has been poisoned by the insidious influence of three facts of life:

➤ Litigiousness

➤ Cynicism and suspicion

➤ "Meism"

LITIGIOUSNESS

The most commonly heard refrain in the pitch of conflict is: "Wait until you hear from my attorney" or some similar not so veiled threat. Likewise, in the minds of most Americans the next best thing to a winning lottery ticket is a promising lawsuit. Litigation and the threat of the same are simultaneously scorned and lusted after by an ever-growing percentage of the population. Those who are disgusted by blood sucking attorneys abhor lawsuits. In the same breath attorneys and resulting lawsuits are lusted after by a society hooked on immediate gratification and instant creation of wealth.

Employees

Employees have grown more and more aware of the benefits of having at their disposal the name of a good attorney. As a tactic for remediation of conflicts in the workplace, this is a card that is more and more frequently played by employees. The middle manager is usually in the path of this threat and must in due course be guarded in all that he does and says. If this threat becomes a reality and results in litigation the middle manager is inevitably the one who will be most exposed in the process to second-guessing and any resulting recriminations.

Customers/Consumers

The threat of litigation from consumers of products is most normally a long distance affair for the middle manager. The middle manager is most exposed to the immediate risk and consequences of litigation from purchasers of services, or what we have referred to here as customers. Customers can reach out and touch the middle manager and they have grown quite fond of the notion that the threat of an attorney during any point of a dispute can produce quite salutary results. Whether as leverage for a desired outcome or as a means to gain a monetary settlement, an attorney in the back pocket is of immeasurable value. Customers not only threaten litigation but they are suing at unprecedented rates.

As it is with employees, middle managers are on the front lines when confronting the threat, or reality, of litigation. The middle manager's actions, or lack thereof, will form an important basis for any lawsuit and the ensuing defense. Again, Monday morning quarterbacks will crawl out from underneath the baseboards and heap recriminations and belated wisdom on the head of the poor guy/gal in the middle.

Bosses

Bosses are pointedly aware of the potential and actual harm that can result from lawsuits pressed by either employees or customers. As a result, bosses respond in a variety of ways to this sometimes real, and oftentimes imagined threat.

One response of bosses is to pursue a cautious course in all things thought about, talked about, or acted upon. This caution can lead to heavy doses of analysis, and deliberation, and cogitation, and interminable processing of the most innocuous of items.

Another response of bosses is to over analyze any and all decisions or actions already made/taken by middle managers. This is especially true if the middle manager hewed to the old adage that it is easier to, "beg forgiveness" than it is to, "ask permission". Likewise bosses can be prone to over analysis when it comes to reactions/responses that emanate from the marketplace (customers/consumers) as well as the work force.

Regardless of the cause of the reaction to the rampant litigiousness, bosses can make the life of the middle manager a living hell. Having to face the threat of lawsuits from two battlefronts represented by customers on the one hand and employees on the other while anticipating and answering the interminable questions from bosses can cause most middle managers to never come out from under their desk.

CYNICISM AND SUSPICION

Cynicism and suspicion creates an outlook on life that has become all too common in the life of America in our current times. These twin heads of the same monster breed a number of behaviors. The most troubling of these behaviors quite possibly is a generalized suspicion of people and institutions including businesses and ultimately middle managers.

Employees

As it related to the workforce, middle managers are in a position, which naturally fosters suspicion on the part of employees. "Management" has at it's disposal the power and resources that employees strive to control and take possession of. When the creeping toxins of cynicism and suspicion enter this naturally adversarial relationship, employees can easily come to believe one of two things.

➢ Any good or positive action undertaken by management is done for an ulterior motive (usually evil or self serving).

➢ Any negative action undertaken by management is done to bring harm or hurt to the employees involved (as opposed to protecting the organization).

The middle manager is challenged with combating the naturally occurring suspicion of employees that stalks their every thought and move.

Customers

Cynicism on the part of customers has grown to pandemic proportions because of the growing chasm between the advertised word and the reality of the delivered goods and services.

Sloganeering has grown to an art form that has fueled a hyper growth in the expectations of consumers and customers. Memorable promises of businesses fulfilling the every dream of consumers and customers, assault our senses on a daily basis. Unfortunately the reality of the service delivered never quite equals the promises churned out by the ad agencies.

This situation is worsened by the fact that that every lapse, insignificant as well as noteworthy, is trumpeted to our collective ears by the cacophonous, ubiquitous media. No story is more celebrated than those involving a business failing to deliver what is expected. The story gains in stature the more the failure is in absolute contradiction to a universally held expectation of something better.

These two realities, unrealistic expectations and the celebration of failures to deliver, constitute two forces plunging headlong toward one another. The force of unrealistic expectations meets the force of inevitable failure at a junction inhabited by the middle managers of the world. It is at this intersection that cynicism and suspicion on the part of customers is bred.

Cynicism on the part of customers manifests itself in many behaviors. Most problematic from the perspective of the middle manager is the mindset of zero tolerance on the part of customers. Zero tolerance is a most prevalent attitude among customers in the business world of today. Zero tolerance means that any lapse in service is inexcusable and nothing can cover or explain away the problem. Further, an attitude of zero tolerance often includes a belief that employees and/or management somehow have conspired to bring about the lapse in service provision. There is no such thing as an innocent mistake or a random occurrence in the mind of the customer who has moved to a position of zero tolerance.

Bosses

Bosses are by their nature questioning and inquiring creatures. In these cynical times, this natural inquisitiveness has devolved into a generalized suspicion of actions, as well as, motives and intentions. Because middle managers are the main interface (some would posit the sacrificial lamb) between the boss and his publics (employees/customers), they are many times caught in the crossfire of suspicion. Additionally middle managers suffer because they can become the target of suspicion and doubt that so muddles the mind of the typical boss of our day.

MEISM

The third unique challenge confronted by middle managers of the ones has to do with society evolving toward a mindset that the individual is not only preeminent but also the exclusive consideration in determining the value of anything and everything imputed by society.

This mindset of egotism or meism is characterized by the belief that any transaction may be governed by the belief that the views, opinions, and beliefs of the individual exclusively govern the resolution of any problem or conflict.

The middle manager's stock in trade is the resolution of problems that develop in an organization. The art of problem resolution is built upon establishing a common understanding of what constitutes an acceptable outcome. In the age of meism, establishing a common understanding of an acceptable outcome is a dicey proposition at best. It is dicey because the parties involved in any conflict have their own view of the problem as well as the solution. Furthermore, they are increasingly disinclined to see what the other party(s) to the conflict are faced with.

In the good day world of the middle manager there exists a natural tension between themselves and customers, employees, and bosses. In addition, there exists a natural tension between each of these three parties.

These natural tensions are heightened considerably by the proclivity of anyone who has a problem to agitate for a solution that meets their needs to the exclusion of all else. The middle manager must divine a way to deal with these natural tensions as well as work to get individuals to see beyond the narrow confines of their needs, wants, and desires. No small task.

Taken together the challenges represented by litigiousness, cynicism and meism create an operating environment that complicates the work of the middle manager on a good day and makes it downright impossible on the all too common bad day.

UNIQUE CHALLENGES

There exist several unique characteristics of the workforce and bosses that pose a particular challenge for the middle manager.

Workforce

The workforce has changed considerably over the past twenty years. The changes have created challenges for all those who attempt to manage in today's environment. The challenges are threefold.

Decimated Supply

The supply of workers in the ones is substantially more constrained than the supply in bygone years. The availability of employees is an issue that impacts every middle manager's ability to carry out the mission of their organization. I would believe that most middle managers would accept the challenge of dealing with any personnel problem other than the one that involves not having enough employees to do the required work. Even with the least motivated, most incompetent of employees the middle manager has a tablet upon which to write a plan to get that person to become a functioning/contributing employee. When there are no employees, there is no opportunity to manage the work/employee equation and the middle manager's job borders on the impossible.

Diversity City

The workforce of the ones has become a veritable cornucopia of humanity. In the old days, the challenge confronting the middle manager was to deal with the issues involving basically two racial groups, and little else. In today's environment the racial melting pot has exploded, littering the work-place landscape with an uncountable number of languages and cultural norms. In addition to this, the number of special interest groups has grown exponentially. The number and variety of protected/special interest groups has grown to the point that cataloguing or characterizing them is near impossible.

Needless to say this creates a challenge for middle managers. The middle manager must manage the relational dynamics between themselves and this diverse workforce. Complicating the challenge is the fact that they must also manage the dynamics between the individual members of the workforce as they interact with one another, customers, bosses, etc.

Dysfunction Abounding

The work force of the ones comes complete with a set of baggage that impacts their ability to be contributing, positive forces in the workplace. The attitudes that eventually manifest themselves range from benign laziness to malignant disloyalty. All of these attitudes are manifest in the work force of the ones.

The middle manager is faced with the task of attempting to deal with these attitudes woven into the fabric of the workforce they are attempting to manage. The task is daunting in light of the fact that "normalcy" in the worker of today is an increasingly scarce commodity.

The unique pressure facing bosses of this day and age is the almost fanatical attention to the bottom line of an organization. This attention has moved from the overall, long term health of an organization to the short term, immediate results that will generate a generous bottom line, a spike in earnings and a buyout resulting in a financial windfall for everyone above a certain level in the organization.

This fixation has created an environment where everything that the middle manager touches has a direct and potentially profound impact on the boss's dream of escaping the work-a-day world courtesy of a precious-metal parachute of one kind or another. This dynamic places the middle manager under the microscope of his or her boss and magnifies every decision and move that is made.

THE MIDDLE MANAGER'S NEIGHBORHOOD

The neighborhood that middle managers inhabit is filled with all manner of dysfunction and twisted dynamics. In total they create a situation that makes the daily battle to survive a difficult proposition. The reality of this situation is often downplayed or totally ignored by those who control the destiny of middle managers. They exist in a dreamy world of possibilities and picture perfect sunsets.

Middle managers who understand the reality of the environment in which they operate are one step closer to the ultimate goal of surviving the middle management experience.

Chapter Three

The Three Pillars of Management

As I have moved through the educational and the actual work phase of my career I have come to identify three separate and distinct tools that managers use to navigate the mucky and miry trenches of middle management. These three distinct tools represent the traditional pillars of modern day management.

The three pillars are:

➢ Management 101

➢ Organizational Policies and Procedures

➢ Legal/Regulatory Structure

Up to this point in the evolution of the art and science of management, these three tools have constituted the entire arsenal at the disposal of middle managers. They are tools with defined strengths, as well as noteworthy limitations.

MANAGEMENT 101

Management 101 is a general, short hand characterization of the body of knowledge, which has flowed from our institutions of higher learning since the concept of management was first born. This body of knowledge is rather extensive and far ranging. It includes traditional management theory in the line of Peter Drucker as well as nouveau theories such as those espoused by such authors as Tom Peters.

This body of knowledge serves a very useful purpose in terms of providing a framework for the study of management. Unfortunately Management 101 fails to always provide practical guidance for the middle manager struggling in a wind whipped sea of ambiguity.

Born of Brilliance

Management 101 is something that flows from the minds and mouths of some very intelligent individuals. No one would ever argue that the ideas, concepts, and theories put forth by the management guru's are not well reasoned, insightful as well as creative. This body of knowledge leaves students of management with a true appreciation for the mental strength of the individuals who have contributed to this area of intellectual pursuit over the years.

Top Down

Management 101 has grown from a variety of sources. However, the majority of theories have flowed from our institutions of higher learning. Professors ensconced in cluttered offices imagining what the world must be like have crafted many a theory about how the world of management works. Likewise, theories have sprung from research that has taken ideas and tested them in the real life laboratory of the business world. In both cases the ideas have flown from the mind of the academician or theorist to the real world situation of the middle manager.

Success Orientation

When on the rare occasion management theories have been generated by real world experiences they have been based on the success stories of individuals or organizations. The thing that sells books and ultimately ideas in today's culture is the story of success (when this success story includes someone getting famously wealthy, all the better). Management 101 is similarly inclined toward putting forward advice and theories for management that revolve around the success enjoyed by a chosen few. With our societal penchant for immediate gratification, we eat up the thought that by photo copying a prescription for success enjoyed by someone else, we too can enjoy that success at a fraction of the expenditure of energy. Success though is the cornerstone of Management 101.

ORGANIZATIONAL POLICIES AND PROCEDURES

Affectionately referred to as P and P's, organizational policies and procedures are as diverse and varied as the businesses they are created to serve and the individuals who create them. Policies and procedures are ideally intended to guide the actions of managers when confronted with a defined set of circumstances. This is particularly helpful when it is necessary to exact consistent responses from different managers across an array of time intervals and situations.

Straight Line

Policies and procedures are very predictable and linear in nature. They are designed to deal with predictable situations in a standard, straight-line fashion.

They are linear in the sense that they follow a standard pattern. A situation presents itself. The manager selects the appropriate policy from his/her ugly, black, vinyl-clad three ring binders filled with policies and procedures. Finding the appropriate policy, the manager reads the policy and almost magically has revealed to him/her the appropriate action to take. The manager then takes the action indicated and is applauded warmly by the adoring masses looking on. The linear form then is: problem recognition/ identification, identifying appropriate policy/procedure, and finally, taking action/affecting resolution. Very neat, very straightforward. Very linear.

Backward Looking

Policies and procedures are for the most part derived from occurrences that have taken place in the past; and that will, with some certainty, occur again, in the future. Their strength lies in the fact that when something happens, as it did in the past, the policy and procedure is there to act as a guide for action to be taken by the manager going forward into the future. This action will take place with the benefit of hindsight that has allowed for the creation of the guiding policy and procedure.

Cut and Dried

Policies and procedures are symmetrical in the sense that for every situation there is a response that is regular, predictable and codified. If a policy is applied appropriately, two different situations will be handled in exactly the same manner. This feature of policies and procedures allows there to be a predictable, consistent response to any situation that fits within the confines of the policy.

LEGAL/REGULATORY STRUCTURE

The legal and regulatory framework, which so permeates the business environment of today, has grown exponentially over the past twenty years. It's growth has tracked with the increasing litigiousness of society and the commonly held belief that any problem in society can be regulated into submission or alternatively remediated by our legal system of laws and courts.

The strength of the legal/regulatory structure in our country is the structure it provides to a whole host of complex and unwieldy situations and settings. As laws and regulations have evolved in our system of commerce they have come to define borders, which in a broad sense define what middle managers can and cannot do.

Laws and regulations tell a manager what he/she can and cannot do at the outer limits of human behavior and discourse. They are by their nature defensive, reflexive and limited in nature.

CRACKED PILLARS

The three pillars of management have definite strengths and at the same time notable imperfections. These limitations are not in and of themselves fatal flaws. However, these imperfections impact on how useful these tools can be to middle managers. Up to this point in time, they have ultimately dictated the survivability of the middle management experience.

Management 101

Management 101 propagates an illusion that any situation encountered by a manager can be solved like an equation by applying the tenets of management theory. Its devotees believe that they hold in their hands the answers to questions that defy description or characterization much less easy solutions.

As was stated earlier in this chapter, management theory is born of brilliant minds. The breadth and depth of the writings in the field of management leave one breathless with awe and appreciation. Unfortunately much of what a middle manager deals with does not come close to the rocket science some management theories would imply. Middle management is so much about the fluid, ebb and flow of human commerce. So much is nuance and intuition and just applying good old common sense to situations that confront a middle manager on any given day. So much is about how to read situations and people that escape easy summarization in textbooks or distillation into a formula.

Management 101 has a tendency toward top down dissemination of knowledge and wisdom. In a theoretical world this would be quite fine. However, the world of the middle manager is far removed from the theoretical abstractions of academicians.

The world of the middle manager is rooted in the real world that he or she works. The middle manager finds the answers to problems on the very site that he/she conducts the commerce of middle management. Solutions are often times imbedded in the facts of the situation confronting the middle manager. Likewise, solutions can spring from employees, customers, or peers. Very seldom do real world solutions, to real world problems, present themselves on the pages of a management treatise.

Finally, Management 101 is built upon the screaming success stories of those in the world of management who have accomplished great things. These darlings of the business world purport to have the keys to similar success for all of the masses of unwashed who would be willing to learn at the feet of these modern day gurus. Nothing succeeds like success, as the saying goes, is an ultimate truism in the world of business.

By way of contrast, the world of the middle manager is one that is filled with an abundance of disappointment and failure. The middle manager will learn manifold lessons from the things that he witnesses being screwed up, as well as the screw-ups he orchestrates himself. For the middle manager the best way to learn is to do. Doing by its very nature invites failure. Therefore, the manager who seeks to learn by doing will certainly experience failure.

The failures a middle manager experiences are personal and can be career and life illuminating. The stories of success trumpeted in management 101 are impersonal and almost mystical. These success stories are ultimately frustrating to those middle managers wallowing in the uncertainty of the middle management trenches.

Unfortunately, stories about struggles, false starts, and failures do not sell well in our modern day society. As a result, middle managers are left with a body of knowledge heavily influenced by success. This is a kind of success that can only reasonably be wrought through the struggles of daily life as a middle manager as opposed to being gleaned from some book.

In general, Management 101 is far removed from the reality of the middle management experience. Management 101 flows from the fountains of brilliance, high above the earthly realms of a middle manager's domain, and light years removed from the struggles and failures that so capture the essence of the middle manager's world.

Organizational Policies and Procedures

Organizational Policies and Procedures are a very useful tool for managers. However, Policies and Procedures are marked by two essential and defining characteristics:

➢ A policy and procedure can never anticipate nor address the endless combinations and permutations that are inevitably imbedded in any situation a P&P is intended to address.

➢ There is no way that a sufficient number of policies and procedures can be authored to address the infinite (in both number and variation) situations a middle manager may be confronted with during a given work day.

Within these defining characteristics lie the essential shortcomings of Policies and Procedures.

Policies are linear and logical and formulaic in how they assist a manager in dealing with any given situation. Unfortunately, very few situations ever go, "according to script". The potential for a situation varying from the black and white of the policy and procedure is overwhelmingly great. The disconnect between the policy and the situation can be great and create apprehension and confusion on the part of any middle manager.

Policies and Procedures can become ubiquitous in some businesses and industries. In health care for example, Policies and Procedures have grown exponentially as organizations such as, <u>The Joint Commission on Accreditation of Healthcare Organizations </u>have become major players in regulating this industry. As I have personally witnessed this explosion of Policies and Procedures I have been humbled many, many times by the emergence of issues and situations that overwhelm the middle manager, much less his ability to author a counterbalancing policy and procedure for each and every conceivable situation.

Policies and Procedures are a tool and they can be a definite aid to the middle manager. However, they are not a panacea and not an answer to a fluid and dynamic environment that mitigates against dependence upon the plodding predictability of Organizational Policies and Procedures.

Legal/Regulatory Structure

Laws and regulations are by there nature intended to define limits upon human activity. As a means to provide boundaries of middle managers, laws and regulations are quite useful. In terms of guidance for managers on how to interact with their environment, laws and regulations are of little help.

Middle management is carried out in a sea of grayness and ambiguity. Middle managers can use laws and regulations to chart out and navigate the outer boundaries of this ocean. However, inside the uncharted waters of middle management, laws and regulations are of limited use because:

➤ The universe of potential situations a manager faces simply overwhelms the available body of laws and regulations.

➤ The life of middle management is forward looking, action oriented, and geared to the unanticipated. Laws and regulations are backward looking, do not generally guide actions, and tend to deal with well-established situations.

Laws and regulations serve a very useful purpose in the world of business. However, as a daily guide to action for the middle manager they are of very limited use. From my experience laws and regulations are often times borne of the joint efforts of attorneys and bureaucrats. Enough said.

FINAL WORD

The three, individual pillars of management have defined strengths and definite weaknesses. Their strength lies in the structure they give to the totally unstructured situation faced by middle managers. Their weakness lies in the fact that in many respects they are removed from the fluidity and perpetual grayness that confronts a middle manager on a daily basis.

The survival of the middle manager is inextricably linked to the tools he/she is able to bring to bear on the situation faced. The tools that have traditionally been available to managers are quite adequate when it comes to predictable, recurring situations that are amenable to time tested, tried and true, formulaic approaches. Unfortunately the survival of the middle manager is inextricably linked to their ability to manage the unpredictable and unanticipated.

Chapter Four

The Big Lie

Clayton, as usual, was working short in the Maintenance Department. Deducted from his four man workforce was one guy on vacation, one guy serving a suspension, and one guy's position going unfilled due to a dearth of qualified applicants.

The winter they were living through had strained manpower as well as the physical plant. Most noticeable to Clayton on that gray, blustery January day was the concrete pad that had heaved two inches in front of a service door. As a result the double set of steel, out-swinging doors had been blocked shut by the raised concrete.

Eddie stumbled upon the scene as Clayton was attempting to manhandle the doors back into position after he had sawed several inches off of the bottom of them. As was his habit, Eddie stopped and gave Clayton a hand.

As they worked, Eddie was struck by the fact that the doors were repaired and reattached with a minimal amount of effort on Clayton's part. He used a sawz all, a pair of pliers and a hammer. With these very basic and simple three tools, Clayton was able to restore this door to fully functional status.

Eddie was struck by the finality of this accomplishment and the fact that those three tools, in and of themselves were wholly sufficient in giving Clayton success in doing what he had set out to do.

Eddie reflected back on his beginnings as a middle manager. Working as an administrator-in-training for a large nursing home chain, Eddie had received in a neat, concise program the three pillars of management. He was thoroughly inculcated to the corporate policies and procedures of the chain. He had hammered into his brain the federal and state regulations that are the source code of the nursing home industry. He had an in-house management guru cull from the full body of management literature the bits and pieces that would make nouveau administrators successful in their first venture as managers.

Eddie came out of this training program able to process payroll and report census, respond accordingly when the state surveyors showed their smiling faces for the annual survey, and divine an understanding about where his Nursing Assistants stood on the Maslow's Hierarchy. He was left with the definite notion that the three tools given to him by his benevolent employer would enable him to conquer any management situation he would ever confront.

Eddie remembered his first assignment after he had finished his training program. The facility he was assigned to as administrator had weeks previously fired their administrator. The Regional Director who introduced Eddie to the facility had told Eddie that he was very uncomfortable with the stability and performance of the number two-position in the facility, the Director of Nursing. On his first and only tour of the facility before he gave Eddie the keys to the kingdom, the Regional Director publicly berated the black, female, and immensely popular Housekeeping Supervisor about the cleanliness of the facility.

As Eddie watched the Regional Director drive out of the parking lot he was left feeling very much alone and abandoned. He had a dawning suspicion that the gift-wrapped, three tools he had received from his new employer would not help him navigate the turbulent waters he would be facing in the coming months. Undoubtedly they would help him do many essential functions of his job. Unfortunately they would be useless as he faced the "soft" issues of people and dynamics and personalities and attitudes and perceptions.

The three tools that Eddie had in his toolbox would not do for him what Clayton's three tools had done for him in repairing and reattaching those service doors.

THE WHOLE ENCHILLADA

Over the course of time as organizational management has become a more defined science; the three pillars have come to be embraced as the definitive solution to the management equation. Those who sit atop the murky trenches of middle management have most warmly embraced this notion.

The firmly held belief is that middle managers who are equipped with the shield of laws and regulations, the breastplate of organizational policies and procedures, and the sword of Management 101 have all of the tools necessary to slay any management conundrum, which might come their way.

This belief has become universally held due to a number of dynamics.

First and foremost, society hates even the scent of ambiguity in the commerce of life. People like to have one answer. True/false. Yes/no. The three pillars of management have come to be seen as the source books, which can provide these definitive answers to any question, or situation, which a manager might confront.

The second dynamic at work is the self-perpetuating nature of the academicians work. As Management 101, in particular, has evolved, academicians have created the illusion that this art of management is reducible to a science. The act of management can be shoved into an equation or assigned a catchy acronym that will somehow magically transform any situation into a self-illuminated, complete answer key for the befuddled middle manager. The worldview of the academicians is that management can be taught and learned in a very objective, scientific fashion. This view assures the continued employment of academicians who focus on management.

The final dynamic at work is potentially the most pernicious. It is the flawed illusion that the three pillars of management constitute the entire array of tools that any manager would need to master the act of managing the human enterprise. This myth flows from the mouths and minds of those who are charged with managing (dare I say controlling) the middle managers of the business world. For the sake of maintaining the appearance of order and control in the face of chaos, those on top of the management heap have no choice but to believe and convince others that management is a very doable, learnable and defined task.

Over the years they have inculcated their management minions with the notion that the three pillars of management are sufficient in and of themselves to allow anyone who is so disposed, to succeed as a manager. To acknowledge that success in management is a very ellusive goal and nebulous concept would call into question their ascendancy to the top of the corporate heap (to which they attribute long hours of hard work and studious application of the three pillars).

Acknowledging that three pillars are not wholly sufficient would also compromise their ability to convince managers under them that success as a manager is attainable by the steady and judicious use of the three traditional tools of management.

REALITY CHECK

As anyone who has ever spent a day as a manager can attest, management is an inexact science at best. Management in its most linear form arrives at imperfect and imprecise answers.

The previous chapter dealt with the strengths as well as the weaknesses of the individual pillars: Management 101, Policies and Procedures, and Laws\Regulations. The individual weaknesses are significant for a manager to recognize and work through as these three tools are used to guide the daily actions of a manager.

However, the individual weaknesses of the three pillars are amplified exponentially when they are collectively embraced as the only tools that a manager will ever need to attain success. The illusion that the three pillars can rescue middle managers interminably wandering in the grayness of the workplace of the ones is pure folly. Beyond folly, this illusion sets the stage for the middle manager to fail more often than he/she will succeed.

Failure as it is being presented in this book does not reflect a determination about blame for the failure. There are ample blame throwers out there hiding in the weeds in the form of upper management types. It goes without saying that blame will eventually, inevitably be thrust upon the bent back of the middle manager. However, for purposes of this book failure can be the result of bad luck, bad timing, bad decisions (middle or upper management), unfortunate circumstances, or just plain old bad karma.

Episodic Failures

As was stated earlier, middle managers will face an abundance of failure throughout their careers. In many cases this failure is of an isolated and situation specific nature.

When confronted with this sort of failure the middle manager responds in a variety of ways. After chastening himself sufficiently, the middle manager that experiences failure will do any number of things, depending upon the nature of the failure. If the failure involved a Management 101 situation he may well run to the bookstore in search of the latest and greatest revelation from the management gurus. Or he may decide that he needs to write a new policy/procedure to address the situation that occurred in hopes of avoiding failure in the future. Finally he might resolve to study more assiduously a regulatory area to know better how to respond to a similar situation should it arise again.

All of these responses to failure are valid and helpful as the middle manager incrementally adjusts his management approach and style when confronting discreet instances of failure. These failures are rarely fatal in their effect on the prospects of continued employment for the middle manager working through intermittent/occasional instances of failure.

Frequent Failures

There are times during every manager's career when failures and problems snow ball. Any middle manager with a modicum of experience and an ounce of honesty will confess that there have been days filled with an overwhelming sense that everything is coming apart at the seams.

When days like these turn into weeks and even at times stretch into months, the middle manager is confronted with failure that will inevitably attract the negative attention of those in the control room of their corporate life. When this happens, the upper management mucky mucks will scratch their heads in dumbfounded incredulity. They will begin the process of meticulously examining the failures and attempt to connect the dots to determine if they are bound together by a common theme or pattern. Generally, this is not a good time for the middle manager.

Cataclysmic Failures

Cataclysmic failures are those instances that are so noteworthy and remarkable that the attention of everyone even loosely connected to the organization or occurrence is inexorably drawn to the show.

This author is fairly well convinced that no industry or business could be more bloated by cataclysmic failures than the nursing home industry. The cataclysmic failures that are so prevalent in the nursing home industry run the gamut of human tragedies. They can include such things as: nursing home resident dies of bed sores…details at eleven; resident wanders from facility and dies of exposure in snow drift…details at eleven; nursing home staff member arrested for sexual assault on nursing home resident…details at eleven.

These are real examples of the cataclysmic happenings that are all too common in nursing homes. However, nothing compares to the annual ritual that nursing homes face called the SURVEY. The SURVEY occurs every 9-15 months and covers a span of 5 days. The SURVEY occurs on an unannounced basis, sometimes beginning on a Saturday or Sunday or even at 3:00 in the morning. The SURVEY team consists of a group of five to seven civil servants. Their job is to compare the facility's operation to federal standards. Imperfect flesh and blood compared to perfectly arranged, black and white standards.

The result of this survey can include citations, civil monetary fines, temporary management, or even an order to close the facility. High stakes stuff to say the least.

With the stakes so high those who rule the nursing home industry have made a part of the annual ritual of the SURVEY, the letting of middle management blood. Cataclysmic failures of this magnitude cry out for a remedy that must include someone's job. That someone is most often the director of nursing or the administrator or quite possibly both.

In general, middle managers that have the misfortune of living through a cataclysmic failure know all too well that the price to be paid for such a debacle is that very middle manager's job.

FAILURE

Failure is a reality that stalks every step that a middle manager takes during his daily walk. When these failures sum up to a critical mass that tips the scales of corporate justice in the direction of terminating someone, the middle manager is most often on the list of casualties

Individuals who have the misfortune of failing as a manager are left with the stomach sinking feeling that their failure is related to some sort of personal shortcoming on their part. The conventional wisdom is that they failed to put the three pillars of management to their best use. As a result they failed on one or many occasions to make full and optimal use of the wholly sufficient tools they had available to them.

REALITY CHECK

In point of fact, the failure of any manager may be related to such things as:

➤ Bad timing,

➤ Bad luck,

➤ Bad decisions,

➤ Poor planning,

➤ Bad karma, etc.

An additional reason for the failure of any middle manager is inextricably related to the perception that the three pillars are entirely sufficient to allow middle managers to survive and ultimately succeed in their calling as a manager.

This universally held perception has had more to do with the downfall of more managers than all of the bad karma a sports team in Cleveland, Ohio could muster.

The three pillars of traditional management practice can be likened to three legs on a stool, a stool intended and designed to be supported by four legs. The middle manager is desperately trying to sit with his full weight balanced on the stool. Believing with all of his might that the three legs (pillars) are capable of supporting his full weight.

After a period of struggle with the three-legged stool, the middle manager realizes that he is never able to balance on the stool for any length of time. He is certainly never able to get comfortable on what for many managers has become a hot seat of incomprehensible and intolerable demands.

INTUITMENT – THE FOURTH PILLAR

Managers who have survived for any length of time have come to realize that the three pillars of traditional management theory are not sufficient to hold the shear weight of the demands of a middle manager's job.

Survival then comes from something outside of the realm of traditional management science. That something I am fairly well convinced is the concept I have dubbed Intuitment. Intuitment is the missing piece of the puzzle that can help assure managers that the traditional tools available to them are woefully inadequate for the task at hand. Most importantly, Intuitment provides strategies, attitudes and values that lend clarity and definition to the pervasive grayness of a middle manager's life. Intuitment enables middle managers to gain some objectivity, improve their performance and maintain their mental equilibrium. Ultimately the application of Intuitment will enable middle managers to survive the middle management experience.

Chapter Five

INTUITMENT - The Essence

Intuitment enables middle managers to grasp hold of the imperceptible rather than stomp all over the obvious.

As has been stated in the preceding chapters, the three traditional tools historically available to middle managers serve a very useful purpose in the structured application of management science. The three pillars are for the most part objective and their application can be universally understood and agreed upon. These tools allow managers the opportunity to deal with concrete, black and white situations in well-defined ways. In a sense the three pillars of management allow managers to stomp all over the obvious. Managers empowered with the three pillars ride with supreme confidence and mastery over the situations that they confront on a daily basis.

Unfortunately for most managers, in most work settings, this ride is rather short and abruptly terminated. It is a ride that ultimately ends with the realization that the three pillars are soon overwhelmed by the ambiguity and variety of situations facing a manager on a daily basis. Situations that escape easy characterization or formulaic answers divined from a book or manual. Intuitment can help managers grasp hold of this imperceptible, but very real, mishmash.

Ultimately, Intuitment can help managers understand and successfully grapple with the imperceptible dynamics that operate within the modern day organization. These are the same dynamics that are imbedded in the hearts and minds of those who regularly interface with middle managers (customers, employees, bosses).

WHAT IT ISN'T

Intuitment is not a panacea, nor a magic bullet for middle managers. Intuitment is built from the actual act of managing. It's growth and development contains a mixture of success as well as failure.

Formula NOT

Intuitment has as a bedrock principle the fact that ninety percent of what a manager confronts on a daily basis is immune to formulaic, standard answers and approaches.

The three pillars of management are primarily built upon the premise of a straight line and the notion of predictability. As the three pillars script it, a manager is confronted with a situation, he/she selects a response from an arsenal of options, slaps one of them on the situation, and magically the situation is solved.

Intuitment is premised upon the immutable unpredictability of situations confronted by managers. Standard answers do not cut it with the endless, breathtaking variety of situations that managers confront. Intuitment does not provide answers so much as it provides a structure for analyzing and reacting to people and situations. It becomes a way of thinking and acting that is woven unconsciously into the fabric of the middle manager's life.

Magical Potion – NOT

Intuitment is not an approach that can be absorbed in a seminar or dispensed in measured dollops of instant wisdom.

So much of Management 101 that spills forth from the corporate bookshelves of our day is predicated on the simplistic notion rooted in our instant-gratification addicted society. The notion holds that the middle manager needs to simply ingest and apply the semi-mystical approaches advocated by the modern day management gurus. In so doing, middle managers will be instantly imbued with a power that will equip them to attain instant success as a manager.

Intuitment, conversely, does not guarantee instant success for the middle manager putting it to use. It allows for the slow, subtle, and even subconscious adoption of strategies that will allow the middle manager to see their world in a different light. Over time these new insights and ways of viewing the management equation will have an impact on the success of the middle manager. Not success in terms of corporate ascendancy or instant wealth. Rather, success in realizing and gathering peace from knowing the defined limitations of management carried out in a world filled with situations that are by their very nature resistant to magical potions and instant solutions.

The Exclusive Province of...NOT

The three pillars of management in general and Management 101 in particular attach great weight to the superstar aura of those who have conquered the business world.

Whether through entrepreneurial or corporate success, those who have risen to great heights in the business world are often times imbued with supernatural powers and abilities. The underlying message is that if everyone in the middle management trenches would model themselves and their lives after the pantheons of corporate America, success would be theirs for the taking. This is the same myth that keeps alive my dream of someday supplanting Michael Jordan's NBA stardom.

However, I will never become Michael Jordan. Likewise, I do not believe that I will imminently fall into a career track reminiscent of Bill Gates. Traditional management thought makes this implicit promise and failing to make it happen is the sole responsibility of the individual manager.

Intuitment, as an alternative, is an approach to management that is available to the masses of middle managers that daily keep the machinery of corporate America operating. Intuitment rejects the notion that success is the exclusive province of those endowed with Kennedyesque qualities or a Jack Welsh penchant for success in the traditional sense of "success" in the world of business.

PURE AND SIMPLE SURVIVAL

Managers confront the specter of success and failure on a continual basis, 24/7. Every interaction, encounter, and situation that a manager faces will yield a positive (success) or negative (failure) result. These pluses and minuses will be placed on some invisible scorecard (visible only to those who rule the world of the middle manager) and be used to determine the ultimate success or failure of the manager whose name is on that card.

More successes than failures for the middle manager leads to permission to return to work the next day (on one extreme) to a ticket to corporate ascendancy in true Walter Mitty style (at the other extreme).

On the other hand a manager who amasses more failures than successes will be the recipient of recriminations, denunciations, criticism and much second-guessing. This will lead to a very uneasy feeling between the middle manager and boss (on one extreme) to an uneasy feeling plus an emptied cubicle or changed lock on the office door (at the other extreme).

The reality of the middle management experience is that ultimate success (corporate ascendancy) and ultimate failure (termination) constitutes an extreme minority of occurrences. For every one thousand middle managers that show up for work on a given day, only ten are promoted or fired on that same day.

The overwhelming experience of middle management is one of daily struggle against a grind of improbability and sameness that tests the shear willpower of every middle manager. At the end of the day the outcome can best be characterized as survival. Survival that allows the middle manager to return to work and struggle anew the following day.

Intuitment is no guarantee of success. It will increase the potential for, and likelihood of success. Most importantly, however, it will lead to survival. Key to this survival is maintaining the perspective that success and failure are fleeting but survival is the Holy Grail for the middle manager. Intuitment will make this survival a certainty by at a minimum maintaining an individual manager's dignity and self-worth.

INTENDED AUDIENCE

Intuitment is an approach to management that in general is targeted at the entire universe of managers. The foundational concepts that underpin Intuitment can improve the effectiveness of anyone who functions as a manager.

More importantly however, Intuitment has evolved into a survival tool for those who consider themselves middle managers. Since the term middle manager is so nebulous I thought that a brief discussion of what constitutes a middle manager might be helpful.

Middle managers are the members of the management ranks who are prone to getting their hands soiled. They are the managers who know the employees by name and circumstance. They are the managers who are faced with the tough jobs of face-to-face discipline. They are the ones who are expected to give of their time and energy in whatever way to make things happen.

For illustration purposes I thought that drawing a parallel between the current day corporate world and medieval times would be most illuminating in distinguishing between middle managers and others who call themselves managers.

Middle managers would be most closely analogized to the warrior class in the feudal world. Upper management would be most easily likened to the ruling class, the aristocracy. Line employees would be members of the working class.

Members of upper management, like members of the ruling class, are endowed with mystical powers over those who live in their kingdom. They have the ultimate and final say over who stays and who goes. They run the show with limited or no accountability for making decisions about little picture items, including who gets to remain in the kingdom. The continuation of their reign as rulers of the corporate world is predicated on such big picture items as corporate profits, stock price, success, etc.

Line employees are members of the worker class. They have very limited power, but equally limited responsibility for corporate goals, success, etc.

Middle managers are members of the warrior class. They are the members of the corporate kingdom who are on the front lines battling to preserve the livelihood of the worker class and at the same time the kingdom of the ruling class. They are warriors in the truest sense of the word. They sacrifice so much of themselves and their identity to make organizations work. They battle against insurmountable odds in a pitched battle against unrelenting, insidious forces, both internal and external to the kingdom organization.

AT IT'S CORE – INTUITMENT

Intuitment as I have defined it is an approach to management that recognizes and acknowledges the distinct limitations of the three pillars of management. At the same time, managers who make use of Intuitment are able to begin to fill the empty void between the promise of the three pillars and the reality of a very compromised, dysfunctional, and uncertain workplace. Through Intuitment this abyss is filled with strategies, attitudes and values (SAV's) that major on intuition and good, old-fashioned common sense.

Intuitment is ideally a mindset, a world-view if you will, that is interwoven into the very core and fabric of a manager's heart and mind. Intuitment consists of a set of values that permeate everything that the manager thinks, says and does during the course of the daily grind of managing. It consists of an overarching set of SAV's as well as specific SAV's for both analyzing and responding to ill defined, totally random situations that managers confront on a much too regular basis.

Intuitment has three major components:

➢ Overarching Strategies/Attitudes/Values

➢ Situation Analysis Strategies/Attitudes/Values

➢ Situation Response Strategies/Attitudes/Values

OVERARCHING STRATEGIES, ATTITUDES, AND VALUES

The overarching strategies, attitudes and values (SAV's) ultimately define who the manager is and what he stands for. They form the bedrock principles that constitute the very core of who the manager is and how the middle manager handles his position and the responsibilities that go along with it.

SELF PRESERVATION SAV'S

Some of the overarching SAV's are aimed at self-preservation for the middle manager. The first four of the SAV's that will be discussed briefly here are ones that are intended to maintain the perspective and ultimately the sanity of the middle manager.

So much of what the middle manager faces is laden with intractable conflict that is in many ways irresolvable at its very core and foundation. This conflict is in many instances twisted to focus on the self worth and value of the middle manager. These assaults can get personal, and more times than imagined, break the spirit and psyche of the middle manager. Intuitment provides a fresh and new way of looking at and analyzing the conflict as well as the resultant, inevitable personal/professional assaults on the middle manager. This view is premised on the goal of self-preservation.

Never Surrender

Never surrender is an attitude and a value that holds sacred the belief that giving up should never be an option. In spite of the grinding sameness, the daily frustrations of managing the human enterprise, as well as the abuse and scorn spewing forth from the Jack Banes of the business world, quitting on the terms of someone else should never be a path chosen by a middle manager. This includes surrender in terms of questioning ones own self worth or surrender in the absolute terms of quitting a job without an exit strategy firmly in place.

The Big Lie

Those who rule the corporate kingdom perpetuate the big lie. The rulers of this world hold that if the three pillars of management are competently mastered and judiciously applied middle managers will reap success by the bushel basket. On the flip side of this heresy is the corporate credo that failure for the middle manager is linked to an inability to understand or appropriately apply the three pillars. This lie is most dangerous and damning for middle managers who invariably confront failure on a 24/7 basis.

Imperfect World/Imperfect People

Possibly nothing can so undermine the confidence of a middle manager than the notion that personal responsibility and accountability extend to what truly lies beyond the finite ability of human beings to control. The middle manager operates in a fatally flawed and ultimately imperfect world. This imperfection is neither his fault nor necessarily within his ability to remediate with any sense of permanence or finality.

Failure, Fait A Compli

Failure is an unalterable, inevitable reality to all who dare call themselves managers. Failure of a situational variety or of a life/career changing variety stalks the every step that a manager takes. Failure indicates absolutely nothing. It is what it is. Failure is meaningful on the corporate scoreboard. To the middle manager it simply means that the battle has been engaged.

While not guaranteeing survival these four SAV's can go a long way toward maintaining an outlook that maximizes sanity and feelings of self worth.

MAXIMIZING EFFECTIVENESS SAV'S

Other strategies, attitudes and values are aimed at maximizing the effectiveness of middle managers. These SAV's allow middle manager's who put Intuitment to use to improve their ability to manage in an increasingly unpredictable business and social environment.

Tuck Your Tie Management

Tuck your tie management (TYTM) is an approach to management that is goal directed and purposeful in its application. TYTM is approach to management that frees the manager to work side by side with employees when not required to because of staffing difficulties. The goal of TYTM is twofold:

➤ Learn how the work is done that he/she is attempting to manage.

➤ Actively display an attitude that no job or any part of a job is too dirty or distasteful or demeaning for the middle manager.

The Synergy of Ideas

Intuitment holds that good ideas are not the exclusive province of those endowed with creative minds. In a similar vein a manager making use of Intuitment understands that recognizing good ideas from an infinite universe is significantly more powerful than the Middle Manager individually pounding out one idea after another in the vacuum of solitary toil.

Balance Good News/Bad News

The manager making use of Intuitment will seek a balance between the smash mouth , confrontational approach to bad news and the very human tendency to procrastinate/gloss over the negatives that so permeate the middle manager's existence. Likewise they will

Major on Organization

The need to manage multiple priorities while simultaneously processing data and information spewing from a plethora of electronic and traditional sources can overwhelm the minds of all but the most brilliant middle managers. Intuitment holds to the precept that the only way to manage this onslaught is through the application of sound, well-planned and purposeful organizational techniques.

Job/Insider Knowledge is Job One

The need to intimately know the industry/business that one is managing is absolutely essential to a middle manager's success. Intuitment establishes this as a major factor in the middle manager's survival. It goes a step further from conventional wisdom by emphasizing that this knowledge is ideally acquired through the eyes and experiential base of employees on the front lines.

Golden Rule

Do unto others, as you would have them do unto you. A simple truism that has underpinned our society for ages. Unfortunately, it has been largely swept away from our society and the world of business on the tsunami of self-fulfillment. Intuitment holds that the Golden Rule and judicious application of common sense should be guiding principles for all of a middle manager's deliberations and actions.

Common Sense

Possibly the most elusive and hard to describe concept in our modern world would be common sense. For purposes of Intuitment, common sense will be distilled down to the middle manager doing the right thing at the right time for the right reasons. The use of common sense by a middle manager using Intuitment will be made possible by their generalist background and bent.

Why Can't We All Just Get Along

The work place of the ones is brimming with conflict. Nowhere is the conflict more evident than in the internecine conflict involving co-workers. Managers using Intuitment are able to identify this conflict and distinguish between the resolvable and the intractable. Intuitment readily acknowledges that much conflict is outside of the power of middle managers to change. However, for those conflicts that are amenable to the control of the middle manager, there are strategies for controlling and channeling this conflict.

Connect the Dots

Middle managers who make use of Intuitment are able to bring their generalist leanings and nature to bear on what appear to be intractable and unsolvable problems. The middle manager who connects the dots engages in actively seeking solutions to work problems outside of the context of the workplace. By moving problems into the context of the wider world managers are able to divine solutions to problems that to most observers would appear to be hopelessly unsolvable.

Foster (Do Not Force) Humor

Middle managers who are able to naturally, unobtrusively and seamlessly interject humor into the workplace create an infinitely more livable environment for employees and customers alike. In the same vein, managers who force humor eventually come to erect insurmountable barriers between themselves and their employees and customers.

Carrot AND Stick

Middle managers who are most effective at doing what they do are able to strike a balance between reward (carrot) and punishment (stick). Human nature being what it is would dictate that individual middle managers have a natural comfort zone and inclination with the stick on one extreme or carrots on the other.

Intuitment calls for middle managers to seek a balance in the use of rewards and punishment when dealing with employees. It is a balancing act that is controlled by situations and organizational policies/culture, but ultimately driven by the mindset of the middle manager. By balancing reward and punishment performance of employees and organizations is ultimately enhanced.

1000 and ONE Ways to Thank Employees

The universe of business literature abounds with how-to-books focusing on ways and means to thank employees. The reality is that middle managers have only one sure way to thank the employees who work with them. That one way is the simple yet monumental act of thanking an employee either in writing or face-to-face. Fortunately for the middle manager there is no other way of thanking an employee that can rival the salutary effects of a genuine, heartfelt "Thank You".

How (NOT) To

The workplace of the ones is overrun with managers who carry out their duties in a less than optimal way. As a result middle managers who only learn lessons from managers who know what they are doing and do the right thing will develop a very shallow experiential base. Intuitment stresses the need for middle managers to learn as much from bad managers and bad management practices as they do from the quintessential good manager carrying out their craft in the best way possible.

SITUATION ANALYSIS STRATEGIES, ATTITUDES, AND VALUES

Intuitment provides strategies; attitudes and values that are aimed at helping managers analyze situations in new and insightful ways. The analysis of situations is critical to the survival of managers who face an unfathomable number of ill-defined, unprecedented, and unwieldy situations.

Situation Analysis SAV's are intended to help managers comprehensively analyze situations with the goal of minimizing doubt and uncertainty while maximizing effectiveness.

That X-Ray Vision Thing

It is important for managers to carefully walk around situations that they confront. The awareness of, and acquired ability to see behind, underneath, and beyond the situation immediately at hand can help managers reduce the doubt factor that shrouds each and every situation and resulting decision.

Manager versus Miracle Worker

Managers confront an overwhelming mountain of issues involving employees that are outside of their ability to control. The manager who puts Intuitment to use is able to discern the people issues that he can control from those that he is powerless to change. In addition, the manager who has internalized Intuitment will focus his efforts on the issues that he is able to control and forego the frustration of playing miracle worker to intractable societal and cultural realities.

Feel Their Pain

Intuitment acknowledges that there is a definite value to managers acquiring and developing the ability to understand the realities faced by employees outside of the workplace. Likewise, Intuitment permits managers to factor these realities into the decisions that are made that impact on the lives of their employees.

Make It Simple Silly (MISS)

The world that we inhabit is complex beyond any one individual's ability to fully and entirely comprehend. While Management 101 champions individual brilliance, Intuitment posits that the most average of managers can take the most complex of situations and break it down into its understandable, constituent parts and solve the equation with alacrity.

Due Diligence

Any analysis of a situation requires that a manager do a proper job of analyzing the facts that surround the matter at hand. This requires middle managers to thoughtfully and completely review the facts of every situation. Managers who use Intuitment will place special emphasis on seeking precedents and getting critical facts in writing.

Internalized Hearing

Managers using Intuitment develop special ability to absorb both the spoken as well as the unspoken word. So many situations that a manager is faced with involve emotions that can obscure or totally bury the facts that are readily at hand. These emotions can so control a situation that they become more of an issue than the presenting problem. Managers who use Intuitment develop an ability to see beyond the obvious and listen to the hidden messages that are inevitably imbedded in every situation.

Don't Sweat the "No Brainers"

Middle managers who use Intuitment develop an ability to categorize the situations that they face. One of the most important situations to recognize and categorize is the one where the response is obvious to everyone with "half a brain". By appropriately placing situations into the "no brainer" category, middle managers leave themselves more mental and emotional energy for situations where the response is not quite so clear and unambiguous.

SITUATION RESPONSE STRATEGIES, ATTITUDES AND VALUES

Managers are so often judged by how they respond to situations. The content of the response matters but so do does the way that the response is communicated. Intuitment helps managers to understand the importance of responding appropriately but also offers strategies, attitudes and value that will maximize the delivery of any response to any situation that is encountered.

Never Fail

The one sacred trust that managers should never violate is the commitment to always respond to every situation and question that arises which involves an employee. Managers are often powerless to control the content of the response to an employee or the reaction of that employee to their response. Managers, however, exercise total control over the simple yet compelling act of "getting back" to an employee who raises an issue.

Timing is Everything

While it is important for middle managers to respond to their employees it is equally as important that they respond according to their own time frame. Managers are captive to many dynamics in their job. However, the one thing that they can exercise control is the timing of their response to an employee. This allows the manager to control the context that the response is provided in as well as every opportunity to fine tune the content of any response.

ID The Button Pushers

The manager is very often at the mercy of the emotions that so pervade the workplace of the ones. These emotions can have a negative impact on a manager when they force a premature or ill-advised response to an employee. At no time is this more apt to happen than when the manager is confronted by a button pusher. Button pushers (and probably their spouse as well) know what issues can get a manager exercised. Additionally, these employees have the proclivity to raise these issues and push these buttons with impeccable timing and great regularity. Managers who use Intuitment develop strategies for identifying and defusing the button pushers that populate the workplace.

Manage WOPT

There is a universal tendency for people to avow with great certitude and tenacity that they do NOT care what other people think (WOPT) about them. Managers are no different in this regard.

The reality is that all humans care what others think about them. Middle managers being first and foremost human can easily get fixated on what employees think about them, especially after they have responded to a situation. Managers who use Intuitment are able to acknowledge that they care what employees in their organization think about them. After this is established in the manager's mind, he/she can use Intuitment to actively manage the thoughts that can negatively influence their response to situations.

Return Serve

Too often managers are surrounded by a cacophony emanating from a flock of problem identifiers in the workplace. An outgrowth of the glee our society takes from celebrating failure and human foibles are employees, bosses and customers who relish an opportunity to point out a problem.

Intuitment is built upon the belief that problems in many instances (especially when they spew from the mouth of a chronic problem identifier) should be bent back upon the problem identifier for potential solutions.

Golden Rule/Common Sense

The final SAV under Situation Response provides four tried and tested truisms for managers to embrace as they respond to situations in the work place:

> ➢ The ability to unconditionally say, "I am sorry", or, "I was wrong".

> ➢ To always affirm the good when pointing out a concern or correcting a problem with an employee.

> ➢ Use the "Boss", "Board", "Corporate Office" as a bogeyman, straw man, or reason for unpleasantness with great discretion.

> ➢ Always treat employees with dignity and respect understanding the good as well as bad angles that are imbedded in the old adage that says, "What goes around comes around".

FINAL WORD

The preceding strategies, attitudes and values are culled from the life and times of one flawed and ultimately failed middle manager. They will be expanded upon in subsequent chapters, replete with anecdotes from pseudo and real world situations.

Intuitment as expressed through these SAV's is not the definitive and final word on the art of management. However, when the strategies, attitudes and values presented here are internalized and put into action by middle managers the results can be compelling. Compelling not only in terms of maximized effectiveness, but most importantly in the maintenance of perspective and sanity. A mental stability made all the more important in a business world with a world-view skewed in favor of customers, employees, bosses and the bottom line.

The ultimate goal of Intuitment and all that it holds is survival for the middle manager in terms of continued employment. Acknowledging that job survival cannot be guaranteed in the best of circumstances, the most important goal becomes that of managers surviving the management experience with their self-image and mental health firmly intact.

Chapter Six

Self-Preservation Strategies, Attitudes and Values

The first four of the overarching strategies, attitudes and values that will be discussed here are aimed at preserving the perspective, self-esteem, and ultimately the sanity of the middle manager. These four SAV's should be factored prominently into the core beliefs and mind-set of the middle manager. They are essential in order for the middle manager to successfully battle the dark and sinister forces that mitigate against the middle manager's sense of self worth.

T-MINUS SIXTY DAYS

Eddie was standing in line at the strip-mall bagel shop with two empty insulated coffee mugs in hand. As we was mentally running through his schedule for the day he could not help but to be struck by the fact that it would be one more day of grinding monotony and gut wrenching problems. Those two realities were equal doses of what Eddie had come to believe was a deadly elixir.

As he surveyed the sea of new and unfamiliar faces behind the counter, his belt clipped pager began to vibrate incessantly. As he read the alpha message his eyes captured the four words that freeze the heart of every nursing home administrator in America. "THE STATE IS HERE.".

These words were all the more ominous because Eddie's professional life extended only from one annual survey to the next. His continued employment at Golden Rule Village was largely contingent upon successfully negotiating this rigorous, largely arbitrary, and entirely gut choking process.

As Eddie went through the checkout line he ran through his mental Department of Health survey calendar. Eddie knew that the State had sixty more days during which they could conduct their annual survey of his facility. If this turned out be "only" a complaint investigation, the likelihood was that the larger stakes, annual survey would occur at the outermost limit of that sixty-day window.

"Mr. Bane," Eddie stammered as he tentatively pushed open the door to the Executive Director's office.

"What is it Travail?" Intoned Mr. Bane's lugubrious voice from the inner reaches of his office.

"Mr. Bane, the Department of Health is here."

Appearing from the corner of his office that held his worktable, Jack Bane placed his fists on his hips and put on a look of utter incredulity. He mocked Eddie with the words, "Welllll? Must I forcibly extract every bit of information from you?"

Reading his mind Eddie replied, "Mr. Bane, sir, I have no idea if this is a complaint or the annual survey. "

"Well Travail, I suggest that you find out post haste. As you are well aware, the corporate office is sending their quality assurance team tomorrow and I had better have some good news for them concerning the outcome of this visit."

"Sir, as always, I expect the outcome to be positive. As soon as I have some information to share I will leave you a voice mail."

Eddie turned away and made a beeline for the conference room where the surveyors would be nesting and prepping for their day's activities. His eyes were greeted by the scowling countenances of two brutish looking women.

Eddie's Director of Nursing was seated opposite the surveyors scribbling furiously as they dictated the information that they would need to have within the hour.

"Good morning", Eddie announced cheerfully to the two surveyors as he extended his hand with a broad smile.

Both of the surveyors barely lifted their expressionless faces from their scattered worksheets as they grunted their greeting.

"Mr. Travail before you ask, this is NOT the annual survey. We are here on a complaint. The complainant, who shall remain anonymous, alleges that Golden Rule has failed to provide a proper diet and is providing residents with dirty and bent silverware.", explained the survey team leader, Mrs. Finger.

Ms. Flaherty and I will be here for the remainder of the day and we will plan to exit at 4:30 p.m. Are there any questions?"

"No, you seem to have covered all the basics. Is there anything else we can do for you?"

"Yes." snarled Ms. Flaherty.

"You will need to arrange to have a test tray sent over for us. We will be dining on the second floor for lunch today."

"Consider it arranged," Eddie replied cheerfully.

As Eddie left the room he had a sinking feeling about the outcome of this complaint survey.

As was arranged, the exit conference happened at 4:30 and the two surveyors took possession of one side of the rectangular conference table. The two surveyors were a picture of bureaucratic efficiency, barricaded behind their tape recorder and laptops, tapping furiously as Eddie and Mr. Bane entered the room.

The survey team leader looked up in the direction of Eddie and Mr. Bane and pulled the glasses from around her ears.

"Welcome Mr. Bane," she said as she forced a smile in their general direction. "Please be seated."

She continued, "It causes me great pain to tell you that our investigation has substantiated a portion of the complaint. Namely, we were able to confirm that residents have received dirty and bent silverware."

Mr. Bane was staring straight ahead as Eddie looked nervously from his malevolent boss to the smirking countenance of the team leader. He could not think of worse "rock and hard place" spot to be in.

"Specifically," she continued. "Resident #3572 received a bent and disgustingly filthy fork for her lunch meal today. Both Ms. Flaherty and I observed this and brought the actual fork with us. Mr. Bane would you like to see the fork?"

"Yes, I would." He exhaled through clenched teeth and lips.

Mr. Bane stood and retrieved the fork from the surveyor. As he returned to his chair he shook his head and gave Eddie that all too familiar look of abject disgust and disappointment usually reserved for his teenage son caught in some unusually despicable act.

"Do either of you gentlemen have any questions?"

"Yes, I do." Eddie replied. "Mrs. Finger I was in the kitchen when the tray for that resident was prepared and I can absolutely say without equivocation that the silverware on that tray was neither bent nor soiled."

"Eddie it doesn't matter what you saw, or say you saw. The evidence is incontrovertible." Mr. Bane began, alternatively glaring at Eddie and nodding resignedly toward the surveyors.

"Well if there is nothing else from you, we have nothing further for you."

Eddie buried his face in his hands and wished for a different life. He thought about how many things had gone wrong with this complaint investigation. He was struck by how much this situation reflected the imperfect world in which he attempted to eek out a daily existence.

IMPERFECT WORLD, IMPERFECT PEOPLE

The situation that Eddie confronted in the proceeding anecdote was a perfect example of the imperfect-world reality that middle managers like Eddie are asked to operate in on a daily basis.

In this case the imperfect world is one where outside forces (the Department of Health) possess a high degree of control, operate with relatively little accountability, and possess the ability to punish individuals and organizations in significant ways. The imperfect people part of the equation was a state surveyor with a vendetta and a resident with a cache of dirty and bent silverware.

The state surveyor had a bad experience with Golden Rule some ten years earlier as an independent, private consultant. The resident was the individual who had called the Department of Health hotline and reported that the residents were receiving dirty silverware. To bolster her allegation this slightly confused and highly vindictive resident had surreptitiously been saving and bending used silverware from her tray for the past four weeks,

Surveyor with a vendetta, meet resident with a collection of dirty silverware. The outcome is obvious and predictable. Could Eddie Travail, or any manager for that matter, have anticipated or avoided this occurrence?

Sometimes our imperfect world, populated with an endless supply of imperfect people, conspires to create difficult and often times irresolvable situations for middle managers. At times like these, middle managers need to keep things in perspective, acknowledge the uncontrollable nature of the world that they operate in, and move on to the next order of business.

This advice is all the more critical when the inevitable denunciations begin to pour forth from the mouths of the rulers of the corporate kingdom. The ruling class will never acknowledge that problems sometimes occur simply because the world is an imperfect place, filled with imperfect people. To do so in their mind would be to create a boilerplate excuse for every incompetent, lazy middle manager whoever sullied the pristine, cut pile carpet of their corporate kingdom.

The walk to Mr. Bane's office was long and chillingly silent.

"Close the door behind you Travail." Jack Bane directed as he made his way to his corner desk littered with stacks of mail and every imaginable periodical. Mr., Bane ripped the glasses from his face and flung them on his desk.

"Sit down Travail." Mr. Bane directed.

Eddie took his usual spot at the conference table that dominated one half of Mr. Bane's office. Jack Bane sank into his leather executive chair and pushed back from the table clasping his large and meaty hands in back of his head

At first Mr. Bane gazed ceiling ward and then riveted his pitiless eyes on the bent and bowed form of Eddie Travail. He spoke in slow and measured words.

"Eddie I have to say that that exit conference was the most disturbing development in my twenty four years in this industry.

Raising his arm to rest on the table, Mr. Bane made a fist and with index finger pointed in Eddie's direction went on, his fleshy face turning a crimson shade of red. *"Never, I repeat never, has this facility, or any facility I have worked in, had a complaint substantiated by the Department of Health."*

Mr. Bane sank back into his chair and continued in a more quiet and superficially calm voice.

"Eddie there are three major points I wish to make with you. First this whole fiasco was totally avoidable. Had you taken any proactive management steps you would have anticipated this situation and taken the necessary steps to see that the complaint was never made or at the very least not substantiated."

He paused for effect, *'Avoidable, avoidable, totally avoidable.»*

Drawing a breath he continued, *«Travail you and I have worked together for many years. I have tried to impart my personal strategies for functioning as a long-term care administrator. You obviously have failed to grasp the treasures that I have laid at your feet. That fact hurts me and it hurts me equally to say without reservation that this debacle is totally tied to your personal failings as a manager and as a man.»*

Swallowing hard and barely drawing a breath Jack Bane continued, *"Travail, I have pulled your personnel file and reviewed it this afternoon. I was disturbed to find that this occurrence is the second such occurrence in the past five years. As a result, I will be issuing a written warning to you. It will be in your E-mail in-box when you return to your office."*

"Do you have anything to say in response to what I have just reviewed with you?"

From previous encounters, too numerous and gut wrenching to recall, Eddie knew that silence was the only acceptable response. Standing he turned and slump-shouldered, shuffled from Mr. Bane's office.

✦　　✦　　✦

FAILURE FAIT A COMPLI

Facts of Failure - There are three:

Failure was an experience that Eddie had grown intimately familiar with throughout his career as a middle manager in the minefield of nursing home administration. In point of fact, failure is an experience that is inextricably linked to the life of the middle manager. Failure stalks the every thought and action of anyone who attempts to navigate the waters of organizational management. To take action, to make a decision, invites the equal opportunity reaper of failure to swoop in and lay bear the heart and soul of those who would attempt to manage the human enterprise.

Intuitment holds that there are three unalterable facts of failure.

1. Failure is Inevitable

Any manager who has ever lifted a hand or a pencil or opened his/her mouth has invited into the equation the inevitable possibility of failure. Managers who do not fail quite possibly avoid this inevitability due to luck. Alternately the manager who does not fail may have alighted onto an organizational perch where action is not necessary and the slow and cautious are rewarded for their very inaction. A final possibility for a manager who does not taste the bitter gall of failure is that the manager may be quite practiced in the art of blaming anyone and everyone for all that goes wrong.

Failure is a fact of live and cannot be avoided. Since it is inevitable, managers should accept it as a reality and something to be met and learned from and embraced as part of the growth process all managers go through.

2. Failure Should Never be Taken Personally

In the real world of business failures can take on mythical proportions for those keeping score on the sidelines. In our society as a whole, and in the world of business in particular, failure is an occurrence and an occasion that tends to draw a crowd. Analogous to a 14-car pile up at Daytona or the personal foibles of a flawed president, failures in the world of business attract all sorts of attention.

This attention tends to make the instance of failure larger than life. As the attention to failure grows, so to does the need to affix a name and identity to the screw-up. It is an incontrovertible fact that bottom line issues are driving business more often than not. As a result those who rule the corporate world want to know who is responsible for failure in a bottom line sense in the "blame someone game".

Once a name has been affixed to a failure, the snowball of personalizing failure begins rolling down the slippery slope upon which the middle manager attempts to pitch his tent. When the snowball hits its mark, the middle manager is eternally connected to the failure. Once this occurs the personalization of failure is a fait a compli.

The institutional personalization of failure cannot be controlled by the middle manager. However, the middle manager can control how the failure is internalized. By a consistent and disciplined approach to failure that accepts its occurrence without allowing it to mark and scar the psyche, the middle manager can depersonalize failure. Learning from failure needs to occur but not at the expense of creating a closet full of negative and noxious memories of past failures and failings. Recognizing the tendency to personalize failure is the first and most important step for the middle manager in managing this obsession with giving failure an identity.

3. Failure should never be kept on a scorecard.

Our society is obsessed with keeping score. The world has become so very keenly aware of who has won and who has lost and what the record is for their favorite, or not so favorite, team, player, or politician. This obsession with the score has spilled over into the world of business.

The corporate world always has, and always will, keep score of individual's performance. Unfortunately the tendency is to etch failure into concrete and let the successes drift off into the abyss of forgotten corporate lore.

The only time this is not the case is when the HR department begins a program to recognize the successes of individuals and departments. Although these are wonderful programs they unfortunately never get woven into the fabric of most corporations.

All too often the approach of the corporate world is to steam iron the record of failure into the psyche of everyone peripherally connected to the failure. In addition the event is recorded in a thousand different places including the personnel folder of the unfortunate, oft maligned middle manager

In spite of this tendency to immortalize failure, middle managers must avoid the natural inclination to keep score. Failures will always occur, are never the personal responsibility of one person and NEVER should be used create some global single number indicator of a manager's worth or effectiveness.

A Little Balance Please

As with the corporate mindset so it is with the middle manager. Too often the good things, the positive acts, the small yet consequential contributions to the forward progress of the organization are never recognized nor celebrated nor entered onto the mental scorecard of most middle managers. When failure inevitably occurs this magnifies the importance of that failure and ultimately does nothing but create doubts and questions in the mind of the middle manager. Once the lesson inherent in each failure is extracted from the experience by the middle manager it should be cast aside in a definitive and permanent way.

References to the failures or failures by mucky mucks are inevitable. If mercy is at all in evidence, the gruesome details of the failure will not be shoved down the gullet of the middle manager whenever the occasion suits the recollection by a vindictive member of upper management. Such retellings of failure should be greeted with respect and deference and then summarily cast aside by the middle manager.

The only exception to this would be when the mucky muck provides an hour for rebuttal during which time the middle manager can recount the countless instances where they have silently and without fanfare saved the bacon of both the company and the mucky muck. Not likely, so get ready to manage, fail, learn and dump.

Failure is truly inevitable. When failure is the result of an activist, thoughtful and sincere effort to bring about something positive in the work environment, it is ultimately a good thing.

Eddie had worked for Jack Bane long enough to anticipate many of his approaches to managing him.

When Eddie received the voice of doom, voice mail, which included the ridiculously early hour Mr. Bane recorded it (no doubt to make Eddie feel guilty for not being at work at the same hour), he knew that a mentoring session was in the offing. Jack Bane, no doubt remorseful over his recent tirades directed at Eddie, asked (directed) Eddie to be in his office at seven o'clock Monday morning.

Monday mornings were tailor made for two things in Jack Bane's world., Mondays were set aside as a time for weekly one-on-one-update meetings with his direct reports to set the misery index in each manager's mind for the coming week. In addition Monday mornings were Mr. Bane's favorite time for teaching and mentoring.

When Eddie arrived the cold chill of the early October morning was blowing full gale through Mr. Bane's office window.

"Eddie, good morning! Please come in and have a seat." He offered effusively from his standing position inside his office.

Eddie was always amazed at how Jack Bane could turn on and off the polar opposites of his borderline schizophrenic personality. He could seamlessly move from a public, verbal flogging of some unfortunate employee to the most convincing good, old best friend routine with someone else in a span of no more than five minutes

As Eddie entered his office Jack Bane was studying the volumes on one of the shelves of his sprawling oaken bookcases. He slowly selected a book and smiled warmly in Eddie's direction. Eddie thought that it was as if Mr. Bane was announcing with his body language, "Come learn at the feet of the Master. Partake of the great wisdom I have accumulated upon these sacred shelves."

Eddie knew all to well what was to follow so he began the process of mentally fastening on his most convincing, eager-student countenance.

"Eddie." Mr. Bane began in his usual monotone embellished with an excited, almost giddy tone to his voice "I have been giving much thought to the predicament you (Mr. Bane always had an innate, automatic knack for framing any problem by using the second person pronoun (you) as opposed to the third person plural pronoun (we)) are facing with the upcoming state survey."

"I am convinced Eddie, that you have within your very grasp the means to slay this state survey dragon."

Turning his attention once again to the shelves Mr. Bane lovingly selected two more volumes and then placed all three on the conference table separating he and Eddie.

"Now you see Eddie I have placed before you the representative samples of the definitive pillars of modern day management science."

"Represented here are some of the best authors in the world of management. I would include yourself in that list as you had a great hand in completing our own Administrative Policy and Procedure manual." Mr. Bane said as he gestured to the massive three ring binder standing bolt upright on the table.

Eddie suppressed a sigh and stared down at the table so as to hide the utter incredulity that was fast burning a hole in his stomach.

Gesturing at the second of the three volumes on the conference table he continued, "This management text is one of the best treatises I have ever read. If you can excuse my highlighting you will find within its pages some of the most lucid insights into management that have ever been penned. I have turned to this volume whenever I have faced a perplexing problem. You may not believe this but the answer always seemed to jump off of the page at me."

"This volume is the latest edition of the survey protocol and it contains all of the regulatory guidance you will need to master this upcoming survey. It is comes replete with surveyor guidance and regulatory interpretations. You will be able to anticipate the actions of the survey team with this magnificent tool. Even though there are over two thousand discrete regulations, you are more than capable of learning it all Eddie."

"Finally, Eddie, this Administrative and General policy and procedure manual is the best guide I could ever give you as you prepare your troops for the upcoming battle with the Department of Health. Contained in this volume is the absolute final word on any situation you will confront as you prepare for the survey."

Mr. Bane paused to catch his breath, as he looked at Eddie with a beatific look of true joy and satisfaction. He was turning over the keys to the kingdom to his loyal subject and he could not have been more pleased with himself.

THE BIG LIE

The ruling class of the corporate world many years ago gave birth to, and to this day, continue to propagate the illusion that middle managers posses the tools necessary to master the world they operate in. The oft times unspoken, yet universal law, is that the middle manager can succeed with the judicious application of the three pillars of management.

The thinking goes that any middle manager that masters Management 101, Organizational Policies and Procedures and the legal regulatory framework will have at their disposal the keys to the corporate kingdom. Conversely, the failure on the part of any middle manager is indisputably linked to the failure on the part of the middle manager to learn, internalize and wisely apply these management tenets.

The shortcomings of the three pillars have been discussed at length in earlier sections of this book. I thought that it might be helpful to illustrate these inadequacies in light of the situation that Eddie Travail was facing, as he prepared for the unannounced onslaught of seven rabid state bureaucrats over the course of four days, all adding up to what they call in the industry the "Survey".

Jack Bane was a manager who practiced what he preached about making use of management writings to guide his actions as a manager. Eddie at the other end of the spectrum was in many senses a front line manager who seldom had the time for quiet, considered deliberation on a matter he was confronting.

So much of what Eddie dealt with had a half-life that could be expressed in nano seconds. Problems would be born and then die within a matter of minutes of one another.

Eddie's stock in trade as a middle manager was to respond to situations and resolve them as quickly as possible. To do otherwise would risk creating an absolute unmanageable backlog of problems and concerns that would quickly bury him under a suffocating heap of vexations. If Eddie used the Jack Bane approach, by the time he solved one problem twenty more would be elbowing their way into his office, quickly overwhelming his ability to function and prepare in any meaningful way for the survey.

This mismatch between the time required to plumb the depths of Management 101 and the time available to respond to multiple situations is but one of the flaws associated with this well-established pillar of management.

Jack Bane's loving embrace of the legal regulatory structure was predicated on the notion that in some magical way the volumes of laws and regulations would sprout legs and conduct the upcoming survey. His world-view held that in some detached, objective way the laws and regulations would leap from the pages of those tomes and apply themselves in a universally understood and accepted fashion.

Unfortunately one of the fallacies of the legal regulatory structure is that those laws and regulations are subject to interpretation and ultimately governed by the individuals who apply them. No amount of knowledge by Eddie could protect himself or the organization from a survey team member with a vendetta or one who happened to be sailing along on a misguided power trip.

Finally, Policies and Procedures are ultimately limited by the complexity of the situations that a manager confronts. In Eddie's world this complexity was at times overwhelming. A Policy and Procedure might define in some very broad context the way to handle a situation. However, they did not begin to touch the gray rainbow of personalities and situations that Eddie confronted on a continuous basis. If Eddie came to rely on Policies and Procedures for the real- time act of management he would be literally writing and rewriting Policies and Procedures on a continuous basis. That process would take time. Time that ultimately was not available. Eddie's time was better spent on the front lines managing the enterprise that was his to manage.

The big lie about the three pillars was one that Eddie had learned not to buy into. He knew that the three pillars gave shape to his formless world but did little else in terms of helping him to survive the details of hand of hand-to-hand combat that his profession often devolved into.

Eddie had learned Mr. Bane's body language like he knew that of his wife. The only difference was that his wife was not a borderline schizophrenic nor was she suppressing an anger problem that would ultimately prove to be self- destructive.

Mr. Bane's level of agitation seemed to be rising as the drop-dead date for the survey drew closer. Most employees took steps to avoid his office and whenever possible change directions to avoid a one-on-one encounter. Eddie did not have this luxury and therefore he could not dodge Jack Bane forever.

When Eddie returned to his office one Tuesday morning he had a voice mail from the voice of doom himself. When Mr. Bane scheduled something, your calendar was irrelevant. However, this message had all of the earmarks of a big time showdown. The tone of Jack Bane's voice left no room for doubt that the discussion would involve a weighty matter and left Eddie's hands sweaty as he pushed the proper sequence of phone buttons to delete the message.

When Eddie arrived for the meeting with Mr. Bane he was called into the office and found Mr. Bane seated as his computer workstation with his back to him. None of the perfunctory preliminaries were spouted from Mr. Bane and Eddie unbidden took his customary seat.

After what seemed like an eternity of hunting and pecking, Mr. Bane turned in his overstuffed leather chair and wheeled himself to the round worktable where Eddie was seated.

"Travail, as I hope you aware we are down to the final week of our annual survey window. I made rounds yesterday and what I found quite frankly disturbs me. I saw so many potential citations that we will be lucky if we get through this survey without an immediate jeopardy finding by the Department of Health."

"Sir, I too have been making rounds and I believe things are in good shape. My directors have been on top of things and I think we will do just fine."

"Well, Eddieeee (said with the same condescension a schoolyard bully would use when taunting someone with that same name), you are certainly welcome to your opinion but mine is the one that counts in this organization."

Pulling himself forward in his chair, resting his elbows on the table and gesturing with upturned, open hands, he continued.

"Travail, it is my assessment that we will have a major problem with the survey and I will be left with no other choice but to terminate your employment at the end of the exit conference next Friday. In light of your eleven years with Golden Rule I am prepared to negotiate your voluntary resignation at this point with two weeks of severance pay."

Eddie had anticipated that it would come down to this. Point of fact he had anticipated it every day for the past seven years. His answer was automatic and well rehearsed.

"Mr. Bane I am not prepared to resign my position. While your offer is certainly a magnanimous gesture I will take my chances with the Department of Health."

Mr. Bane's face convulsed with anger and he crowded the table even more. The upturned peace offering hands had turned into pile driving forefingers aimed at Eddie's face.

"Travail, you have made your choice and you will live with it. I hope for your sake you have chosen wisely. You are free to go."

NEVER SURRENDER

Too often the world of the middle manager is filled with situations similar to the above. The stakes are so high and the casualty list is long and sprinkled with the bodies of middle managers who decided it was easier to throw in the towel than come back out for another round of face pounding.

The fourth and final SAV aimed at the self preservation of the middle manager is the one that places the highest premium on maintaining control of the employment situation as long as possible and whenever possible.

There are times when the destiny of a middle manager, whether he remains employed or not, is not in the direct control of the middle manager. At times such as these the rulers of the corporate kingdom take control of the destiny thing and make suitable arrangements for desk clearing and office lock changing before the middle manager has an opportunity to utter words of protest or self defense.

At other times the decision to remain employed or to "voluntarily" leave the employ of an organization is entirely in the hands of the middle manager. These two distinct situations place the middle manager in the position of making a decision about whether to leave or stay.

The Voluntary Termination Ruse

In the voluntary termination ruse the middle manager is presented with a golden opportunity to resign before the organization is left with no choice but to terminate the hapless middle manager. This situation can be complicated to the max by offers of severance arrangements, future job references, etc. However, in it's most bare bone's form as depicted in the anecdote above, middle managers who succumb to this offer are often placed in the position where their destiny is dictated to them and where they are at a distinct disadvantage. When this is the case, surrender is never a good choice and should be resisted at all costs. Had Eddie Travail accepted the meager and miserly offer from Jack Bane, he would have had practically nothing to show for all of his years of loyal service to Golden Rule. Given the outcome of the survey he would have in fact unnecessarily surrendered a job that was at a minimum providing a living for his family.

The Path of Least Resistance

The pressure of always being ultimately accountable for the success or failure of a venture is a wearing experience. When this natural pressure is accentuated by the unrelenting demagogic style of an abusive boss, the daily grind takes its toll from a psychological standpoint. Eddie was a manager who toiled under the unrelenting grind of unrealistic expectations spewing forth from the mouth of a bombastic, haranguing, heartless boss.

The toll from working under these conditions can manifest itself in things such as involuntary hand tremors, facial twitches or a whole host of gastro intestinal maladies. When the toll exceeds a manager's ability to cope he/she can be pushed to the point of throwing in the towel and quitting a job WITHOUT an exit strategy in place. In situations such as these, the situation has taken control of the manager and as a result the manager has reduced his opportunity for a wise career move to zero.

In the absence of something that approaches a golden parachute, the middle manager should never surrender to a boss dangling a conflict free, voluntary termination. Similarly middle managers should never succumb to the temptation to walk away from a nasty job situation without a plan in place for continued income.

EPILOGUE

The survey team arrived on the Monday morning following Eddie's meeting with Jack Bane. As the script called for, the survey team descended like a swarm of carpenter ants on a wet and mushy piece of plywood. Eddie was almost relieved. For this one week the distinction between friend and foe would be clearly delineated. The survey team was the enemy. Eddie and his people were united in their resolve to exact a good outcome out of this arduous process. This week was unlike the fifty-one other weeks of the year in that the battlefield was plainly established and universally agreed upon.

As fate would have it, Golden Rule had a very good survey. The survey team leader was firmly in charge of the process and not driven by hidden motives or a pathological undermining team member with a hidden vendetta/agenda.

Eddie felt a transitory vindication. He was comforted by the fact that he had negotiated an imperfect process, confronted and accepted failure, relied upon his own instincts rather than the three pillars, and finally had not yielded to the temptation of easy surrender to an implacable foe.

Eddie's job was intact for the short term, his options for seeking another position while gainfully employed was secure, and his belief in those who worked for him rock solid. Ultimately he had lived to fight another day.

✦   ✦   ✦

Chapter Seven

Maximizing Effectiveness SAV's Externally Focused

The next group of strategies, attitudes and values is concerned with increasing and ultimately maximizing the effectiveness of the middle manager. This chapter will concentrate on SAV's that are externally focused. They will improve the performance of the middle manager when interacting with the outside world and especially with ubiquitous personnel issues and problems.

These SAV's are of particular importance because the most fatal flaw of the three pillars of management science is their static nature. When this flaw is juxtaposed with the unalterable fact that human beings and the relationships that flow from daily discourse are immutably fluid and infinitely variable, the middle manager is most in danger. Only an approach like Intuitment can bring hope to managing these dynamics and increasing the likelihood of the middle manager's success and survival.

Golden Rule

The golden rule as I learned it goes something like, "Do unto others as you would have them do unto you." It is one of the underpinnings of our civilized world. Throughout history it has become the glue that has held many societies together. Unfortunately it is an adage that has lost most of its currency in the corporate world (if it ever had any in the first place). Too often the need to succeed and win at all costs has made the corporate rule and the golden rule mutually exclusive propositions.

There are of course exceptions of an individual and corporate nature. These exceptions are usually individuals who are nominated for boss of the year and organizations that are regularly judged to be the best places to work.

The golden rule as exercised by middle managers is an axiom that is critical to their overall and long term effectiveness. On the receiving end of decisions and pronouncements from middle managers the workplace of the ones holds the golden rule in very high esteem. In a passive sense employees are constantly judging managers to see if they live by the, *do unto others, as you would have them do unto you* credo. Among more aggressive and judgmental employees middle managers are overtly and actively taken to task when their actions fail the golden rule test.

Whether judged on an active or passive basis the credibility of middle managers is inextricably linked to how their workforce judges them with respect to their adherence to the golden rule. Middle managers who behave in a callous and indifferent fashion will have a workforce that is thirsting for middle management blood. Employees will not have any sense of loyalty to such a manager and those who are so inclined will actively plot and scheme for the demise of that individual.

Blame and credit represent the two sides of the same coin. Most situations that occur in the world of business generate a coin toss resulting in either blame or credit. The golden rule would posit that managers should be judicious and circumspect with the dispensing of credit and blame. Too little of the one and too much of the latter will lead to a disgruntled and eventually mutinous work force.

Intuitment promotes the notion that taking blame when blame is unassignable is far superior to spreading blame. Managers who make use of Intuitment when faced with a negative situation or problem that cannot reasonably be attributed to an individual or a group of employees will take the blame for the failure upon himself. This is not to say that the manager needs to become the company scapegoat. Managers need to be forthright and direct when dealing with situations and willing to acknowledge and deal with employees who are responsible for failures.

However, there are times when stuff just happens or failures are the result of a systems breakdown that cannot be traced to any one individual. In instances such as these, middle managers need to be willing to accept the yoke of ultimate accountability and take the blame. Managers who are not using Intuitment and most concerned with their own agenda and performance scorecard will do whatever is necessary in terms of giving blame to ward off the fetid stink of failure that can doom the opportunities for their personal advancement.

Likewise with the concept of credit, managers who have internalized Intuitment are inclined to give credit where credit is due. Insecure managers will always be reluctant to give credit lest the person being given the credit usurps their position or looks better than the manager in the eyes of the mucky mucks. Managers who are comfortable in their own skin will always take the opportunity to give credit to their subordinates who do something right or noteworthy.

In summary the Golden Rule of Intuitment relies upon managers giving credit (where credit is due) and taking blame (when blame is of an indeterminate origin). Adherence to this rule will in no way guarantee success in the short-term sprint to the top of the corporate heap. However, abiding by this precept will allow the middle manager to establish credibility with those who ultimately determine their long-term survival and success.

Why Can't We All Just Get Along

Conflict is as much a part of the modern day workplace as it is the world in which we live. It is so ingrained in the workplace and in people's notion of what it means to be a fully functioning and engaged human being. Conflict takes many forms and has many origins. This book will not seek to explain the totality of conflict but rather to acknowledge its presence and provide strategies for dealing with this unalterable part of the management equation.

I have seen conflict throughout my work life. Conflict between individuals in the work force seems to be an immutable law of human nature. Some basic facts need to be understood and internalized before conflict can be adequately managed.

First and foremost conflict is unavoidable. The presence of conflict is not a negative reflection on the competence of any middle manager. Likewise, the absence of conflict does not confer upon the manager who happens to be in the vicinity the title of super performer. Conflict is an outgrowth of the fallen nature of our human race. Managers are not responsible for the fallen state of man and likewise should not take personally the fact that conflict exists in their workplace.

However, managers do bear a great responsibility for recognizing and ultimately confronting conflict that exists between members of the workforce. Conflict between employees that is either not seen/recognized or ignored by middle managers will grow and become a festering boil on the face of the organization. Ultimately it will undermine the credibility of the manager and lead to organizational problems that are not amenable to easy correction.

Recognizing conflict is an art that develops over time. It requires middle managers to take in the whole gamut of human behaviors. The key is to listen and to observe. Nothing can replace a middle manager listening and observing and most especially when they are in the presence of employees who are showing signs of being at odds with one another. Human nature makes us all want to avoid situations and people that are brimming with the potential for conflict. However, it is essential that the middle manager actively seek out opportunities to be in the presence of employees even when those situations might be rife with the potential for conflict. The purpose behind drawing oneself into these situations will be to learn whether or not conflict exists and if it does what the nature of the conflict might be.

Confronting conflict is one of the most difficult things for a manager to do. It is always easier to avoid situations that are rife with conflict. Managers are generally able to find an infinite number of things to do other than deal straight on with conflict between two or more employees. However, nothing can more quickly unravel all that a manager works for than unchecked conflict.

Once a manager has decided to intervene in a conflict between employees the possible approaches are limitless. This is not meant to be a treatise on conflict management so I will begin and end this section with one main and essential suggestion for dealing with conflict between warring employees.

Second, only to the inertia involved in managers staying out of conflict is the temptation to do anything and everything except actually arranging to have the combatants sit down at the same table with the middle manager as the referee. Taking the initiative to have people who may in fact hate each other to sit down and talk openly and honestly is a step that is fraught with danger. There are no guarantees that the embattled employees will end the meeting by embracing each other. Sometimes a manager is simply thankful a fistfight did not break out.

However, in all of my years of experience as a manager I have come to be convicted that face-to-face confrontation is the best way to handle conflict between employees. The middle manager by taking the always bold move of arranging for warring employees sit down at a table in a neutral location with the purpose of discussing their concerns demonstrates in a clear and convincing fashion that they are not afraid to face the conflict. The employees from their perspective realize that the middle manager has acknowledged the conflict and put the employees on notice that they will share in the responsibility for resolving the conflict. The monkey of unresolved conflict has been deftly moved from the back of the middle manager to the backs of the warring employees.

In spite of a middle manager's best efforts, conflict is sometimes not amenable to resolution. In cases such as these the goal of the middle manager is to minimize the disruption and the potential damage that can accompany conflict between individual employees.

In one of my past work experiences I had two front-line supervisors who were very capable and strong willed individuals. They both ran their areas with aplomb. In spite of my best efforts and multiple counseling sessions with the three of us they never resolved their conflict. In this situation it boiled down to the fact that they respected and liked me as a person and a manager more than they hated each other. I believe that this fact alone made their relationship work and allowed them to contribute to the forward progress of the institution that employed us all. At times this is the best that a middle manager can hope for.

In as much as conflict is an immutable law of organizational dynamics, the existence of conflict is never the fault of the middle manager. However, it is always incumbent upon the middle manager to seek to recognize and address the conflict so that at the very least the conflict is contained or possibly channeled in constructive ways.

Balance Good News/Bad News

The world of the middle manager is filled with an abundance of information to take in, process and act upon. This information can be divided into two basic categories; good news and bad news. Managers being creatures of habit sometimes tend to stress either good news or bad news when they are interacting /communicating with those they manage. There is nothing inherently wrong with one or the other. However, the tendency to stress one over the other can lead to discouraged/disenchanted workers (too much bad news) or deluded/clueless employees (too much good news).

I have worked for and observed the actions of managers who seem to believe that it is their mission in life to deliver a never-ending stream of condemnations, criticisms, problems and shortcomings. For managers such as these the glass of water that is sitting upon the workstation of their employees is always half empty. There is always something that is not up to standard and therefore the manager feels compelled to bludgeon the face of the worker bee until the mercy rule kicks in (Don't you wish that as employees we could invoke the mercy rule when the never ending string of criticism reaches a critical mass and we can stand it no more) or the manager tires of beating the motionless corpse of their underling.

The tendency to share nothing but bad news undoubtedly has many motivations. Some managers probably believe that by sharing bad news and constantly raising the specter of the worst possible outcome they are doing their part to keep their employees always on the edge of maximum performance. They believe that by sharing a preponderance of bad news they keep their employees from becoming complacent and lazy and taking things for granted. Unfortunately this approach does nothing but deflate and ultimately destroy the psyche and spirit of those in the work force who are subject to an unrelenting stream of bad news.

Likewise, sharing nothing but good news creates a false sense of security and sense that everything is just peachy. Managers who communicate good news to the exclusion of bad news create in their employees a false sense of reality. My experience has been that managers who oversell the good news are either in denial themselves or deathly afraid of the reaction of their employees to bad news. Many times this tendency to over emphasize good news is driven by the fact that we are overwhelmed at times with the bad news that so permeates the world of business and main street USA.

A manager who makes use of Intuitment is a manager who is able to strike a balance between good news and bad news. He is able to use the good news to encourage and bolster the morale of his employees while using bad news to frame the reality of the business and work environment they are operating within. A manager who is able to dispense measured dollops of both good and bad news will reap the reward of a balanced, informed, and motivated workforce.

Tuck Your Tie Management

Tuck your tie management is a central tenet of Intuitment. It is an approach to management that holds sacred the belief that any job or discreet task that is under the control of a middle manager is a job or a task that he/she knows how to do and willingly embraces the notion of performing that very task or job. Tuck your tie management is goal directed and purposeful in its application.

Many times in the life of a middle manager, they are called upon to perform the duties of someone who is working under them. This can be for a multitude of reasons. With the recent shrinkage in the supply of workers and the undependability of those who are hired, the middle manager is often pressed into service to fill a void. At other times the middle manager seeks to perform the job of someone under him to avoid doing the stuff of management that they find distasteful. Neither of these situations (staff relief or seeking the safety of menial tasks) are what tuck your tie management (TYTM) is all about.

Tuck your tie management is an approach to managing that places a premium on consciously scheduling time and seeking opportunities to perform jobs and tasks that the middle manager routinely supervises. It has two major goals:

❖ Learn at a very basic and practical level how jobs are actually done and how they interrelate to other jobs, departments, etc..

❖ Actively display an attitude that no job is too dirty, dangerous, base, demeaning or distasteful for the middle manager practicing TYTM to carry out.

Middle managers are very often called upon to step into the breach of operations when someone calls off sick or a vacant position goes unfilled. This is the nature of a middle managers position. This is usually not an ideal time to practice TYTM as the middle manager has not done this in a planned way and most likely has one eye on the job that they are filling in for and one eye on their job, which due to the unplanned nature of the staff relief role is going undone. Additionally, these are the times when operations are stretched and the ability to observe a normal workload and work situation is most likely not possible. Likewise, some managers enjoy doing the jobs of folks under their control because these tasks are less of a burden than the stack of work that awaits them in their office.

Tuck you tie managers are those who actively plan times so that they can spend time engaged in jobs and tasks in their area of control. They do this not out of dire necessity or because they are seeking an escape from the tortures of their manager's role but because they want to know how things are done on a normal day under normal circumstances. TYT managers are managers who eventually are able to perform the majority of the tasks they are supervising. This knowledge is indispensable as a manager grapples with issues of work performance, productivity and the general structure and functioning of an operational area. TYT managers are ones who know the names faces and stories behind the workers who keep their unit functioning. They can observe firsthand all of the dysfunction and anomalies that may or may not exist between members of the workforce. They are able to identify problems before they happen.

There is a second reason for TYTM. That reason is not as obvious as the first reason but no less important to the success of a middle manager.

Eddie Travail worked in a retirement community. By their nature, retirement communities that have a healthcare component can have some very base and undesirable jobs that are part and parcel of nursing home operations. Eddie was not a nurse or a trained nursing assistant. He was a distant cry from anything approximating a health care professional. However, Eddie Travail was respected by his staff from the most educated professional to the lowest paid entry-level employee. His respect was earned and mutli-dimensional in nature. One of the

things that his employees recognized and would unanimously acclaim was that Eddie was not afraid of any job at Golden Rule Village.

There was one story that followed Eddie around that had to do with a resident's pet on the Assisted Living unit. Residents were encouraged to have pets and one of the residents had a dog that was the favorite of residents and staff alike. Unfortunately like his owner this dog was aging and loosing control of some of his bodily functions. This dog was increasingly unable to distinguish between the outdoors and the indoor hallways when nature called.

One morning, Eddie was accosted by an irate, dog-hating housekeeper who was spitting about this geriatric dog leaving a mess down the middle of the hallway. Eddie was on the scene in minutes and determined that this was an out of the ordinary occurrence and an ideal opportunity to show that nothing was beneath him. Grabbing some paper towels off of the housekeeper's cart Eddie went down the hall with steely resolve and picked up each and every one of the dog droppings. A small thing in terms of time and energy but a big thing in terms of making a statement of what Eddie was willing to do. A story that was repeated many times that day as much to criticize the dog-hating housekeeper as to marvel at the fact that the guy in the tie was willing to do such a chore.

By virtue of the fact that Eddie showed he was not above a task such as picking up doggie droppings, he was able to gain in no small measure the respect of those he worked with. This kind of respect will serve middle managers across a broad range of situations and be something remembered longer than one could imagine. Situations like the one that Eddie confronted cannot be fabricated nor can they be orchestrated. When situations occur where managers can step out of their box or comfort zone they need to seize them with no thought about the reaction of employees or subsequent spinning in the break room.

Tuck your tie management seeks opportunities to do things that are outside the ordinary role of the manager. These things are done in order to learn, become more aware of what is going on and demonstrate an egalitarian approach to the operation of their enterprise. When Intuitment is in full force and used to its fullest extent, managers have their tie tucked a great deal more than they have it dangling jauntily from their neck while perusing the current issue of Business Week with their feet propped on their desk.

Carrot AND Stick

How to motivate employees is a conundrum that has no definitive answer. The manager who makes use of Intuitment is one who is able to meld the best of the "carrot" and the "stick" approach to motivating employees.

The "carrot" is representative of the approach to management that rewards employees with positive things to encourage them to perform their job at ever higher levels of proficiency and capacity. The goodies range from a pat on the back to positive commendations to additional pay to promotions. The "carrot" as a motivator is limited by the size of the basket of goodies and the imagination of the middle manager creating new and exciting ways to reward employees.

The "stick" is an approach to management that holds that employees can best be motivated by fear. Fear of a disciplinary note, fear of termination, fear of recriminations, fear of conflict. Fear is a strong motivator and can be very effective in motivating employees to perform their job. It can be a viable approach in the short term but is not overly effective in the long run as employees eventually tire of such an approach that relies on negatives. Employees who toil in such a situation, either shut down, have a nervous breakdown, or simply move to another job to escape the dysfunction inherent in working for a boss who uses the "stick" to the exclusion of the "carrot" to motivate employees.

The three pillars of management seem to pinwheel the middle manager from the one extreme of the "carrot" to the other extreme of the "stick". Policies and procedures and the legal/regulatory system encourage middle managers to use the objective, no nonsense "stick" approach to motivating employees. The "stick" is generally objective and does not generally call into the human relations equation any subjective judgment on the part of the manager. Policies and procedures as well as laws are tailor made for straightforward, unambiguous situations involving employees and typically favor the use of the "stick".

The management gurus seem to push the middle manager to the other end of the continuum. The latest and greatest management treatises promulgate innumerable approaches and ways to reward/motivate employees with all of the creativity that they can dig up from the work places of the ones. The ideas are gleaned from corporations all across America and poured onto the pages of management how-to-books that middle managers can read and copy, ad nauseam.

Internal issues may also drive managers who use the "carrot" or the "stick" exclusively or predominantly in their management dealings. Wielders of the "stick" may feel most comfortable in the black and white box that treats employees like mathematical equations that they need to solve. At the other end managers who use the "carrot" exclusively may be frightened by the conflict that is inherent in using the "stick" when dealing with employees. Managers who manage at the extremes of the reward continuum will either have a cowed and angry workforce or a workforce that will never have its fill of perks and pats.

Managers who use Intuitment recognize both the strengths and limitations of the "carrot" and the "stick" when dealing with employees. They are able to move from using the "carrot" to using the "stick" in a seamless and comfortable fashion using whatever means to motivate employees that suits the situation or the employee involved. Their employees are most likely to have a balanced and healthy view of what the workplace can and cannot provide to meet their psychic needs. They will not cower in constant fear that the hulking and captious Jack Bane-like creature in the form of their boss will arrive at any moment to lay waste to their self-esteem, or livelihood, or both.

Foster, Do Not Force, Humor

The workplace of the ones is a setting that cries out for the therapeutic benefits of humor and levity. However, humor is a delicate undertaking. One person's humor is another person's justifiable provocation for a fistfight.

Middle managers who make use of Intuitment make humor a priority in the work place. They are constantly, consciously seeking to create an environment that fosters humor and light heartedness. Many times humor is the only possible antidote to the oppressiveness of the workplace of the ones. Middle managers should keep in mind four cardinal rules when attempting to interject humor into the workplace.

➤ **Humor should always be contextual.** Middle managers should attempt to sew the seeds of humor by seeking opportunities in the normal flow of the work day. Laughter and light heartedness that is borne of two or more people sharing something humorous is a blessing for those sharing the laughter as well as those within earshot.

Possibly the most difficult humorous device to make contextual is the telling of a joke. Too often jokes can offend people in ways that can never be fully anticipated. Additionally, jokes told by a manager will most likely elicit laughter from the employees they are told to. Although some of the laughter generated by jokes will be genuine a percentage will be nervous laughter borne of the rule that subordinates laugh at their boss's jokes. It is this nervous, insincere laughter that flies in the face of efforts to make laughter a genuine, normal and universally welcome experience in the workplace.

➤ **The inside joke is one of the best types of humor.** When managers live their work lives with their employees they develop a sense of shared history and experiences. This history inevitably begets tremendous grist for inside jokes. These jokes can take an oppressive and intolerable situation and magically transform it into a source of laughter. This humor not only lightens the spirits of all those who partake but binds the middle manager to their employees in subtle but very compelling ways.

➢ ***Humor at the expense of another is the worst kind of humor.*** At all costs middle managers should avoid using humor that takes advantage of individuals or groups of individuals in the workplace. This destructive sort of humor is all too common in the workplace of the ones as well as in our society as a whole. It is easy to create humor at the expense of another and can be entertaining beyond words. However, in spite of the short-term laughter that reverberates off of the office walls, it will result in hard feelings on the part of those who are the target. Finally, even those who may be laughing will wonder when the middle manager will eventually direct this nefarious brand of humor at them.

➢ ***On the opposite side of the deprecating humor continuum lay self-deprecating humor.*** This is the sort of humor that can be very effective in leveling the playing field and establishing common bonds between he middle manager and employees. The middle manager should not aspire to become the butt of jokes. However, self-deprecating humor when properly controlled and judiciously applied can put a face of humanity and approachability on the middle manager who makes use of this humorous device.

Humor is an important element in the workplace of the ones. Middle managers that are able to foster humor will improve the productivity and attitude of the workforce. In addition the days will not seem so long and the task of managing so daunting.

One Thousand and ONE Ways to Thank Employees

Several years ago I was given a book that outlined a plethora of ideas for thanking employees. They were all gems of ideas, each one brimming with creativity and suffused with workplace transforming possibilities. Of course I was immediately suspicious. It seemed that simply plucking a recipe for a thank you from this book, tweaking it a bit and dropping it into the lap of an employee would never adequately communicate the message of gratitude that is imbedded in the worldview of middle managers using Intuitment.

Traditional approaches to management tend to view expressions of gratitude to employees as a purely reactionary gesture. This would typically unfold in the following fashion. An edict floats down from the overlords at the corporate office on the importance of thanking employees. The E-mail would include instructions for surveying employees and developing an annual plan of some sort to make sure that employees felt as though they were appreciated.

In the short run this would serve to make employees feel like they were appreciated. Unfortunately with the coming and going of corporate personnel and programs there can never be any guarantee that thanking employees will continue to be a corporate priority supported with time and resources. Likewise employees of the ones are imbued with cynical and skeptical minds. They are quite suspicious of gratitude that is insincere or the least bit contrived.

Intuitment holds strongly to the belief that thanking employees should be something that is interwoven into the management style of the middle manager and by extension into the fabric of the enterprise that he/she is leading. It has three core principles for creating a work atmosphere where employees feel truly appreciated for what they do.

Intentional/Heartfelt

Middle managers making use of Intuitment have imprinted on their hearts a spirit of gratefulness. Their expressions of gratefulness for their employees are always in evidence. This gratefulness arises from a basic understanding that above all else the success/survival of the middle manager is tied to the efforts of those people who work for him/her.

Middle managers express their gratitude acknowledging that if things go well for them and their enterprise they have their employees to thank. Expressions of gratitude that arise from a heart that is humble and filled with a true sense of thankfulness will make the most basic thank you something that will warm the soul of most employees.

Intentional and heartfelt gratitude cannot be manufactured or orchestrated from an external source. It must arise from the mind of the middle manager as he/she sees and acknowledges that their employees are the source of every good thing that takes place in the world of work.

Consistent

Those managers who use Intuitment embrace the need to say thank you to their employees 24/7, 365 days a year. Expressions of gratitude will flow from the middle manager to employees regardless of the external or internal environment. It is quite easy to let opportunities to say thank you slip by as internal organizational dynamics and realities crowd out the time and resources necessary to say thank you.

Intuitment driven managers will make the act of saying thank you an absolute imperative. If resources are not available for a big splashy thank you, then a simple thank you note will in fact happen. Likewise if their organization is going through turbulent times, the middle manager using Intuitment will dig down and find the energy necessary to say thank you.

Personal

Middle managers should always place a premium on personalizing any expression of gratitude. Spoken words are always appreciated but when a manager takes the time and effort to thank an employee in writing the impression and impact is magnified to a significant degree. So much of our communications are transient. From interminable cell phone talk to text messaging, communications have been so stripped of permanence as to have little or no meaning. In such an environment a written note takes on such greater importance and has a much more long lasting impact on the receiver.

In terms of thanking employees there is one (and only one) can't miss way to express gratitude with meaning and substance. That one way is to either tell the employee face-to-face "Thank you for…" or to express the same sentiment in writing.

Expressing gratitude to employees is truly a 24/7, 365 day a year endeavor. Alone it is not a guarantor of success. However, it will do as much as anything in terms of building a sense of loyalty among employees toward the middle manager. Ideally it will move them to want success for the middle manager as much as they want it for themselves.

Looking Outward

The above strategies, attitudes and values that are focused on the outside world are not the only ones that a manager has at his disposal. They are SAV's that I have found to work in my life as a middle manager as well as in the lives of managers I have observed throughout my career.

While they in no way guarantee a manager's survival they do form the basis for managers functioning more effectively as they interact with the world around them. A world that is ever changing and always challenging.

Chapter Eight

Maximizing Effectiveness SAV's – Internally Focused

MAJOR ON ORGANIZATION

Mr. Jack Bane was a collector of management treatises. He had every book under the sun of the corporate world. He actually read these books with great regularity and tried desperately to apply what he learned. However, in spite of his penchant for trendy knowledge accumulation he was all-together too human and a far cry from a perfect manager.

This was never more evident to Eddie Travail than the one day he was being lectured by Mr. Bane for failing to follow up with him on something or another. Eddie was taking his dress down in silent submission and praying for deliverance from the wrath of Jack when the lightning bolt of irony struck Jack Bane's office.

"Travail you need to get yourself more organized. You will never succeed until you master the art of being organized at all times and in all things."

With that, Jack Bane began to dig through the four solid oak shelves that lined one of the walls of his office. He rummaged and mumbled and muttered as he searched with increasing desperation for this book that would deliver Eddie from the disorder of his life. Unfortunately (or fortunately) Mr. Bane never did find that book on organization. Eddie was released from one of his many brow beatings and allowed to return to his world of middle management where solid oak bookcases are not the norm and the luxury of using books to guide one's actions is precluded by the immediate need to act and react and manage on the dead run.

Eddie never did get that book but he had an intuitive sense of the importance of organizing his work life. This organization spanned everything from how he managed his day to how he organized the seeming endless reams of paper that came across his path during the course of his job.

Organization is a competency that is indispensable to the middle manager. Those who occupy the upper floors of the corporate world have many tools available to them to help manage their work-a-day world. These tools range from computer based programs to the latest greatest handheld PDA's to personal consultants who will come in and help organize the office of a harried executive to small armies of administrative assistants to assist with the task of day-to-day organization. The world of the typical middle manager is not afforded these same luxuries of time and resources. The middle manager must rely instead on a more basic, intuition-driven approach to organization.

The deluge of information and data is overwhelming to the senses of most middle managers. This never-ending cascade of information in every imaginable format creates many challenges for the middle manager. The middle manager needs to assimilate, organize and store the information for purposes of decision-making and problem solving. Failing this, the middle manager is destined to be set adrift in a sea of confusion. Soon the overwhelmed middle manager will be utterly lost in a raging vortex of paper, computer files, and voice mail/E-mail messages.

This book and this section are not meant to be a guide on, "How to Get Organized". Rather it is meant to be a clarion call for all middle managers to acknowledge the compelling need to be organized. Middle managers who seek the holy grail of organization need to have as an underlying premise the understanding and acceptance that no human being is capable of absorbing, processing and making use of all of the information that is potentially at his/her disposal.

This acknowledgement of a managers finite abilities flies in the face of popular images of fast track business executive types who pride themselves on the ability to handle multiple tasks and manage a deluge of E-mails and voice mails and snail mail and memo's and trade publications and every sort of communication. They are held up as the model that we should all aspire to. They wear their pagers, cell phones and PDA's with a smug hubris. No doubt very similar to prehistoric folk who trumpeted their prowess as hunters with flashy displays of skins and pelts at the entrance to their cave.

Unfortunately, the super achieving and death-wish-driven business executive is not the target audience of this survival guide. Rather it is geared toward individuals who happen to be managers and want to have a life outside of work and sanity within their world of work.

Organization for the middle manager without huge resources at their disposal nor a wish to be totally immersed in their work environment relies mightily on the ability to eschew the temptation to absorb every nugget of information that comes rolling in the office/cubicle door. Managers who make use of Intuitment develop the ability to make conscious decisions to delete, throw out, tear up or toss out (sometimes without reading) electronic and hard copy material that has no discernible bearing on, or connection with, their job at hand. They do this regularly and religiously to keep their desk, voice mailbox, E-mail box and ultimately their mind clear and uncluttered.

In addition to throwing out, middle managers who wish to organize must develop a system for organizing their priorities, their projects and the people who report to them.

Organizing priorities is concerned with the ability to organize both current/day/weekly activities as well as the long term-activities. There are many approaches to managing a middle manager's to do list. Primary among them is the discipline of the manager to make certain that items are recorded on a short term or a long-term list, as they become priorities for action. Secondly, priorities must be either addressed and crossed off of the list or moved to the long-term list or consciously discarded because they are no longer priorities. Items must never be allowed simply to languish on the daily/weekly list for more than two weeks or simply drop off because of laziness or inattention on the part of the middle manager. The failure to follow-up or follow through will lead to the damnation of a middle manager faster than any other sin of omission or commission.

Organizing projects can become an all-consuming pursuit for middle managers. There are entire seminars devoted to the subject of project management. Obviously this is a multi faceted topic and one not amenable to over simplification. The only thing that I have seen in my career that has benefited me in the area of project management is the pocket style manila folder. I have found that these unassuming folders are the ideal catchall for the endless streams and snippets of information that are given birth to by projects. Information can come fast and furious to the harried middle manager and it can be misplaced or lost with the greatest of ease. The ability to have all of the information in one place allows managers the luxury of finding the information that is needed or requested by a superior. The simple act of having some information available is tremendously powerful especially as so many others are drowning in the same sea of confusion and paper.

Managing people can be a great challenge for the middle manager. A manager can have many people who he must remain current with on issues, projects, and people that they may supervise. One thing that is helpful when managing people is a running list of issues, projects and people that need to be discussed with each individual reporting directly to the middle manager. The list need not be exhaustive or detailed but should provide an outline for productive discussions that will provide a snap shot of where things stand with all of a middle manager's direct reports. In addition, any employee who has a follow up list in the hands of the middle manager should be met with on a regular and ongoing basis. Too often in the hectic world that is the life of a middle manager, contact with direct reports left to chance will result in a disconnect that can seriously impair the functioning of all involved. Happenstance meetings will not allow for the regular, predictable and productive two-way exchange of information.

Organization is a SAV that is critical to the success of any middle manager. The art of organization is not something that is amenable to formulaic, one-size-fits-all solutions. Organization is something that has to be adapted to the variables of the person, position and organization. Even though there are no pat approaches to organization, the middle manager that makes use of Intuitment recognizes the importance of organization, actively seeks to bring organization to his/her priorities, projects and people, and is constantly experimenting with new approaches to the exigency of being organized.

Connect The Dots

The second internally focused strategy, attitude and value is what I refer to as Connect The Dots. Connect The Dots is a strategy for bringing solutions and insights to bear on a problem or issue in one field with solutions from a different and often times distant or totally unrelated field or sphere of activity.

Middle managers more often than not are defined by what they are NOT. Middle managers are NOT accountants. They are NOT human resources specialists. They are NOT normally technical specialists. They ARE generalists in the purest sense of the word. In a sense their greatest weakness is part and parcel of their greatest strength. Their weakness revolves around the difficulty of defining what a middle manager is. It is a decided strength, however, in terms of a middle manager's tendency to possess interests that span a wide array of fields and subjects.

Middle managers by necessity need to acquire knowledge in a wide range of disciplines. Even though they are not accountants they need to have a passing knowledge and proficiency of how accounting systems work. Even though they are not human resources specialists they need to have a grasp of how the basics of human resources functions. The list of disciplines goes on and on. This need to know much about a wide variety of subjects reflects a mind set that middle managers either enter the profession with or adopt as a survival mechanism over time.

This mind-set is one that disposes the middle manager to always seek to acquire information from a wide range of topical areas. This proclivity to seek to know many things about many different subjects is absolutely key to a manager being able to connect the dots.

Connecting the dots is never more important than when a middle manager is confronting an intractable problem or situation that seemingly defies solution. These are problems that can continue for such a long period of time they become a part of the fabric of the organization. The middle manager is so inured to these problems that they no longer see them and they become accepted as a fact of life. Managers who are able to Connect the Dots can draw from their most salient defining feature as middle managers, their generalist bent, to look at these problems and situations with a fresh set of eyes.

Middle managers who are confronting intractable problems or situations need to remove them from the context of work and expose them to the light of a different scene. This means carrying the problem home and reflecting upon it as the world outside of work occurs. This does not mean carrying the problem around like some sort of millstone weighing down every minute of the middle manager's every day. Rather it should be carried ever so lightly in the recesses of the middle manager's mind and brought out as he/she lives out their life outside of work with one goal in mind. That goal is to find a solution or part of a solution that can move the problem from a fixed and unchanging part of the landscape to something changed for the better.

By removing unsolvable problems from the organizational context that comes to define them, the middle manager is able to overlay the problem situation or person upon the full range of life experiences that he/she experiences outside of the world of work.

An example would be a longstanding employee who has evolved into an extreme undercurrent in the organization. This employee by virtue of their seniority and ability to outlast every boss they ever had, has taken on an air of invincibility that has protected them from the disciplinary actions for all manner of performance issues. The middle manager with the misfortune of managing this employee could quite easily come to view this situation as an unalterable fact of life and resign him/her self to simply manage around them. Unfortunately this does not solve the problem. Equally as clear is the fact that the solution to this problem employee has not been found within the context of the organization.

The middle manager confronted with this situation and making use of Connect the Dots approach would do well to transport this employee and their unique characteristics from the work context and overlay them on as many situations and contexts as he/she comes in contact with outside of the work environment.

The middle manager might well envision how Joe Torre might handle the forty homer guy with an anger problem, or how the CEO of a Fortune 500 company might handle a back stabbing vice president. The middle manager might even see something as they observe their spouse deftly handling their rebellious seventeen-year old son. He might even glimpse the pathology of this employee when alighting on the Springer show while channel surfing one afternoon. He might see something in the self -destructive nature of the Middle East conflict that casts a different light on the issues that this problem employee is confronting.

The awareness of the importance and the ability to connect disparate fields and situations to the real life unsolvable problems of the middle manager can open up whole new insights and potential solutions in the most improbable of ways. The alternative for the middle manager is to render intractable problems invisible (to their eyes only) or alternatively to allow them to fester to the point that they become a source of eternal vexation and begin to consume the life force of the middle manager.

Connect the Dots draws on the most defining characteristic of a middle manager, namely their generalist bent. This generalist bent allows middle managers to apply the full range of their life skills and interests to what others consider unsolvable problems. This new way of looking at problems can minimally preserve the sanity of the middle manager and quite possibly lead to new and exciting solutions to old and stagnant problems. Both outcomes will contribute mightily to the long-term survival of the middle manager who is able to Connect the Dots.

Job Industry is Job One

The middle manager that is fully utilizing Intuitment acknowledges the need to maintain an insatiable appetite for remaining current and well versed in the dynamics and happenings of the industry that they happen to work. This desire to continuously acquire knowledge and information is an essential ingredient for the middle manager to maintain his ability to navigate the waters of the industry they work in. This is particularly the case in industries that are experiencing change at a rapid pace.

Eddie Travail was one such manager. He worked in the field of long-term care and the change that this industry confronted was always fast paced and driven by the regulatory environment that so permeated the business. It has been said that only the nuclear power industry has more excessive regulatory oversight than the nursing home industry.

Eddie was unfortunately not a model for the importance of a middle manager always seeking to keep abreast of current happenings. Eddy's heart was not in keeping up to date with the changes that were always afoot with respect to regulations and reimbursement. He had been a nursing home manager for many years and whether due to the demands of the job or the domineering taskmaster he worked for, Eddie had lost his desire to continue to grow professionally in long-term care administration. Eddie was in need of new job, or a career change, or both. By allowing himself to slip further and further behind the knowledge curve, Eddie was setting himself up for eventual failure borne on the wings of his own neglect as opposed to a whimsical termination at the hands of Jack Bane.

As a counterpoint to Eddie I am reminded of my cousin Tom who has made himself into a snack food baron of some note. Along with his mom, dad and brother Bob they have taken a fledgling potato chip distributor selling chips out of a casket warehouse to a multi million-dollar manufacturer and distributor of all sorts of snack food items under the Grand Ma Shearer's label. Several years ago I had the opportunity to tour their huge production facility and was in absolute awe of the scale and scope of their operation.

What also made a great impression on me was the knowledge that Tom exhibited while he gave me a tour. His area of specialization was sales and marketing. However, he had every snack food industry trend and fact at his fingertips as he showed off what has to be one of Ohio's, if not America's, penultimate rags to riches success stories. When we finished the tour, Tom expounded about the future of a paperless delivery system for vendors who service grocery stores. His fervor and keen interest in this subject was quite obvious and really demonstrated a love for, and an interest in, the industry that he was clearly riding heard over.

Contrasted with Eddie's lack of interest it was easy to see why my cousin's engagement had translated into such dramatic career success.

Middle managers must dedicate themselves to mastering industry knowledge for a number of reasons. Major among then is the simple fact that there are simply too many ways to get fired as a middle manager. So many things can wrong that are totally out of the control of the middle manager. Staying abreast of current industry trends is controllable and directly related to the survivability of a middle manager. It can additionally help the middle manager in his career progression and maximize his employment options.

Synergy of Ideas

Throughout my career I have been struck by the great value that is placed on individuals who possess creative minds. More valuable than gold are employees who have an imagination and a creative spirit. When this is combined with knowledge in a particular field, the owner can parlay the combination into a fully paid trip into the heavenly realms of the corporate kingdom. New and fresh ideas are the fuel that fires the corporate machinery of this and every decade.

Intuitment is an approach to management that accepts the value of creativity, imagination, and new ideas. However, Intuitment holds firm to the precept that there is one thing infinitely more powerful and valuable than an ability to generate new and creative ideas. That one thing is the ability to recognize good ideas that are generated by others.

If given a choice between an ability to have a creative mind or the ability to recognize good ideas in others, the manager who practices Intuitment will always choose the ability to recognize a good idea in others. Intuitment holds that the idea generation potential is increased a thousand-fold by the simple act of soliciting, sorting through, and recognizing good ideas that spew forth from the mouths and minds of others in an organization.

Recognizing the ability of others to generate ideas is a far superior resource to the most creative mind of any one individual. The middle manager that uses Intuitment to seek out and recognize the good ideas of others is creating synergies that will benefit not only the middle manager but the entire organization as well.

Too often the mystique of the creative mind has been used to make those who might lack creativity to feel inferior and inadequate. Creativity is undoubtedly a special gift and in fact it may not be able to be taught or learned. However, the manager who develops an ability to recognize a good idea (regardless of the source) and at the same time trains his ego to allow others the opportunity to shine a little bit with the recognition that inevitably accompanies a good idea will be immeasurably more successful than a creative manager who only recognizes his own ideas as strokes of brilliance.

Intuitment also holds fast to the belief that the individual who generated the good idea should receive proper recognition and reward. It is so tempting for a human being to NOT give credit where credit is due. I am sure that the conflict raging in a manager's mind goes something like, "If I give Charlie the credit for this idea, my boss will probably wonder why he needs me."

This is a fear that a manager must come to grips with. If a manager falls into the trap of failing to give credit where credit is due, or worse takes credit for ideas that were the creation of someone else, he/she will find that the well of ideas and solutions emanating from his/her employees will dry up.

As was stated earlier in this book, Intuitment is premised upon the fact that management is NOT the exclusive province of the brilliant or those who are most well endowed with the proper academic and social pedigree. Intuitment holds fast to the belief that ordinary individuals can do immeasurably more and better with the proper mind set. Part of this mind set is developing the openness to the ideas and creativity of others. Managers who do this will excel in ways that will eclipse the performance of the self-proclaimed geniuses of the business world.

The anecdote from earlier in this book was a perfect example of the beauty and power imbedded within the synergy of ideas. Eddie Travail was a manager confronting a very unique situation. He was desperate for an inspiration that would divine a solution to the leaking roof conundrum and deliver him from the unforgiving and withering wrath of Jack Bane.

Eddie considered himself to be a fairly creative individual. He was generally able to generate ideas and solutions to problems where none seemed possible at first blush. His favorite saying in this regard was, "Desperation is the mother of invention." The situation that he faced with the inordinate amount of snow on the roof of the building quite frankly had him stumped. He was not experiencing any lightning bolts of insight that would lead him to a solution. He may have been put off by the time critical nature of the situation or perhaps he simply felt powerless to fight the circumstances and forces of mother nature that were obviously stacked against him.

Whatever the cause of his dry well syndrome, Eddie knew the critical value of tapping the minds and creative resources of others. He did just this when he seized upon the suggestion made by a non descript, uninvolved dining service's employee. The idea formed the basis for a solution to Eddie's unsolvable problem. By making use of this idea, Eddie was delivered from his dilemma and given a chance to return to work the following day. There need be no doubt that whenever Eddie was asked about this situation he would celebrate the genius of that employee by name and give him all of the credit that his idea deserved.

How (NOT) To

Human beings take on many and varied roles throughout their lives. From child to sibling to parent to teacher to coach to manager we all wear an abundance of hats and take on a variety of roles. Part of the process of rotating into new roles is the tendency to observe and critique how others carry out the roles that we have played in the past, the ones we are currently playing, or those we will play in the future.

I am certain that everyone can recall saying something like, "When I'm a mom (dad) I will never treat my kids liked they do." Or similarly, "When I become a coach, I want to be just like Mr. Jones." The process of critiquing and analyzing how others function in a known role is universal.

The same is true when it comes to those who occupy the role of middle manager. By virtue of their position in the middle, middle managers have ample opportunities to observe how other managers at their level as well as bosses handle their role as manager.

The picture that a typical middle manager sees, ain't always pretty. Quite the contrary. Managers see a disproportionate amount of, "How NOT To" manage examples as opposed to examples of "How To" manage. This is due to an abundance of factors that have been touched on throughout this book. However, the bottom line is that in vast stretches of the world of management the phrase, "best practice" is almost an oxymoron.

Intuitment holds that managers who are blessed to witness good management practice should take advantage of all opportunities to learn and adapt those practices to how they carry out the art of management. Likewise, and so much more importantly, middle managers need to consciously strive to learn from the ubiquitous examples of bad management. This includes management practices that they are the target of, as well as those, that they observe that are directed at other unfortunates. There are two very simple, yet compelling, reasons for managers to always learn from the "How NOT To" examples.

This first reason is especially true when the middle manager is the direct target of bad management practice. As anyone who has been trapped in a dysfunctional relationship can attest, the natural and first tendency is to become embittered. The bitterness that springs from the manager being the brunt of cowardly, incompetent, dishonest, or abusive management practices will eventually consume the very soul of the middle manager. Along the way the manager will stop being effective in their role as a manager.

Secondly there are way too many examples of "How NOT To" manage and way too few examples of "How To" be an effective manager. Managers that only mirror the examples of good management that they experience will have a very shallow base of experiences from which to draw as situations present themselves. They will be consigned to never grow as managers beyond the bounds of what they learned from the few good managers they have been blessed to observe or work with. Since there are way too few good managers, the middle manager who only learns from the good examples will be left with a hollow experiential base ill suited for the multitude of situations that are faced in the course of a "normal" day.

Managers can only grow by learning the "How To's" as well as the "How Not To's" of management. By failing to actively and constructively build upon the deluge of poor management practice, middle managers will inevitably be forced to repeat these sins. Bad management has many causes. One of them must certainly be the failure to learn from the sins of the past. However, when the bad is turned into a positive life lesson and results in a personal resolve to handle the same situation in a better way when the opportunity presents itself, the cycle of bad management propagating bad management is broken. This is when managers become better managers and the world of work becomes a more habitable space for everyone involved.

Common Sense

In the world of traditional management, managers confront a world that is very black and very white. Their worldview holds that any situation that they confront has an answer in a textbook, a policy book or some tome of laws and regulations. Their need for common sense is minimized to a great degree by virtue of how they view and respond to their world.

Conversely, managers who embrace Intuitment see the world as a sea of gray ambiguity. As a result they come to rely on common sense to help them navigate these unchartable waters. The world of the middle managers that I know and respect is filled with situations and decisions that have no prescribed, preset, predefined answer or approach. Theirs' is a world of unknowns and unknowables that render decision making a challenge that is best confronted with helping doses of common sense.

Common sense can mean a thousand different things to a thousand different individuals. For purposes of Intuitment it can be distilled down to doing the right thing at the right time for the right reason. Because of the fluid nature of the middle manager's field of operations, the ultimate decision about what constitutes the right thing at the right time for the right reasons may ultimately boil down to what that little voice inside tells the middle manager to do.

Whether you call it a gut feeling or intuition or that little voice inside of you, middle managers come to rely upon this internal guide whenever they are confronted with a situation where their response is not obvious or prescribed in a policy book or law/regulation.

Fortunately middle managers generally live their lives among the people and over time come to know what it is to interact with all strata of society. Likewise they come to experience most every conceivable situation in their work lives. They see and hear and most importantly experience all that work life and real life has to offer. By virtue of this exposure to people and situations they develop an ability to intuitively know how to read people and situations. This eventually becomes the little voice inside of each of us that speaks the language of common sense.

The common sense of middle managers grows not only as a result of their lives but will increase exponentially as they continuously confront the challenges that the world of work presents. Their inner voice will gather wisdom from situations that they observe around them as well as decisions that they make (good and bad) over time.

Summary

This chapter has focused on internally focused strategies, attitudes and values. They are linked by the common goal of increasing the effectiveness of everything that the middle manager touches during the course of a day. They are for the most part built upon a foundation of common sense and core values that place a great emphasis on viewing problems and situations with an eye that is ever searching for answers in places that are discounted by human pride and the arrogance that sometimes accompanies ascendancy into the hierarchy of organizations.

These SAV's will provide a peace of mind that moves in lockstep with organization, a firm base of knowledge and the ability to look to others as well as strange places for the answers to organizational problems and issues. The goal of this chapter as well as this entire survival guide is to maximize the opportunities for the middle manager to survive in terms of his psyche as well as in terms of his career options. These SAV's have at their core the concept of common sense and all can be easily integrated into the practice of management once a conscious decision has been made by the middle manager to embrace the practice of management in new and hopefully better ways.

Chapter Nine

Situation Analysis

The only thing that is more important than a manager's response to a situation is that manager's analysis of that same situation. Situation analysis is the starting point for any manager faced with an operational, organizational or personnel situation that he/she must respond to.

Situational analysis is the process of critically analyzing and examining a situation so that all that can be known about the situation is known BEFORE the manager responds. The goal is to reduce the unknowns to the lowest possible number so that the information at the disposal of the manager allows for the most informed and insight-filled decision possible.

Situation analysis also relies upon a world-view that is heavy on common sense and an a priori assessment of people and organizational dynamics. It requires middle managers to scratch below the surface of any situation to uncover the underlying issue that needs to be considered as a part of any solution. Situation analysis, if done correctly and completely, will provide the basis for well reasoned, fully informed decisions.

That X-Ray Vision Thing

As middle managers move throughout their careers they must consciously and consistently work to develop an ability to look beyond, behind and beneath the situation that presents itself to their naked eyes. This is an ability that can be fostered by understanding that in many situations what is at first discerned with the senses may not be the entire story. Intuitment is predicated on a manager intentionally looking beneath, behind and beyond the situation that is immediately before them is a key strategy.

This is so critically important because so much of a manager's time can be spent dealing with the same situation over and over again. Dejavu all over again because the manager engages in a repeated exercise of reacting only to the situation as it appears on the surface. Typically this is an effort to get things off of the "to do list" by moving quickly and decisively to address the situation at hand. Unfortunately failing to look beneath, behind and beyond a situation can result in frustration, additional work and a feeling that the manager is stuck in a low budget version of <u>Ground Hog Day</u>.

The ability to see beneath a situation is based on the understanding that the situation at hand may not be the real situation. The operative question for the manager who is practicing Intuitment is, "Is their something underlying this situation which is the real root of what I am perceiving?" Is the employee evidencing a behavior that is in response to something else in his job, the workplace, or his life outside of work? The manager who can discern the root problem underlying any situation that he/she faces will be light years ahead of other managers in terms of their ability to remedy the situation in a successful, conclusive and ultimately final fashion.

The ability to see behind a situation is linked to a desire to determine if the situation presenting itself is in someway inextricably and critically linked to another employee, department or issue in the organization. The manager who addresses situations in isolation from how they connect to other parts of the organization is, again, setting themselves up to eternally revisit the same issue. In addition, managers who fail to look behind a situation are potentially creating more of a mess than they could ever hope to solve with a superficial analysis of the attendant combinations and permutations of a situation. Looking behind the surface of an issue may create complications but will always maximize the opportunity that a solution is a final and complete.

The ability to see beyond a situation is tied to a manager's inclination to manage for the short term. It is so easy in today's immediate gratification world for managers to solve problems with an eye only on making it through another week of employment.

Seeing beyond involves the manager at the very least considering the future in relationship to the situation immediately before them. The recognition that the situation that is dealt with today can have implications on future events is a key component of a manager's analysis of a situation. The ability to see these potential ripple effects without allowing decisions to become an exercise in analysis paralysis will take practice and can often times only developed in the crucible of experience. Suffice it to say that managers, who look beyond the immediate situation when analyzing a situation, will spare themselves or the organization significant grief down the road.

A manager's credibility is enhanced significantly by the ability to solve problems and address issues in a final and definitive fashion. By looking beneath, behind and beyond the situation at hand, the manager exponentially increases his/her opportunity for success. A success borne of careful and deliberate analysis of situations will be of a more permanent nature than can ever be accomplished by the simple knee jerking, autopilot responses to the next item on the, "to do list".

Manager or Miracle Worker

Middle managers are always confronted with situations that revolve around the performance of an employee. The quandary that I have often found myself in when confronting an employee performance issue is assessing the chances that the performance issue can be successfully addressed and the employee salvaged.

In the finite realm of time, a manager must decide when and where to spend his or her limited resources of time. In this regard no task can be more time consuming than dealing with employee performance issues. When time is spent ill advisedly, it is not only wasted time, but wasted effort and emotion as well. Deciding when to work with an employee and when to move on can have a direct impact on the performance and ultimate success of the middle manager.

A manager who makes use of Intuitment is able to utilize a construct for assessing the ultimate potential for successfully solving performance issues of employees. It is a construct that attempts to place employees in one of four boxes. Normally it is not a good thing to place employees, or people for that matter, in boxes. Unfortunately if a manager does not have some way of objectively assessing the ultimate potential for successfully working through performance issues with employees, time will be wasted and ultimate failure pre-ordained.

Throughout my career I have been struck by the fact that employees distinguish themselves in two essential and important ways. First, employees distinguish themselves with respect to their ability. This revolves around the employee's ability to understand the basic elements of a job and perform that very job to a high degree of proficiency with limited supervision and intervention. Secondly employees have always stood out in my mind in terms of their attitude. I know that attitude is nebulous and a manager should avoid focusing on attitudes. For the sake of this paradigm I believe that a judgment can, and needs to be made, with respect to the employees' attitude. Attitude in my experience is tied to such things as ability to get along with others; willingness to learn new things and accept new responsibilities; and generally a positive cheerful outlook on life.

GAT/GAB – Good Attitude, Good Ability. This is the kind of employer that every manager covets. They can make even the most mediocre of managers look a lot like Peter Drucker. They are individuals who distinguish themselves with a can-do approach to any task put before them. They are positive in their approach to their job, the organization and the people around them. They are also employees who have an ability to get the job done. They learn quickly, need little direction and supervision and always find a way around problems and issues that arise. Middle managers who are blessed with GAT/GAB employees are tempted to "hug their neck" every morning that they arrive for work. They are a breath of fresh air and a joy to behold and be around.

When the GAT/GAB employee has a performance problem they have probably in most instances identified the problem themselves, taken the necessary steps to correct the situation, and probably been harder on themselves than the manager could ever be. Performance issues, when they exist are addressed quickly and for the most part not repeated in the future.

BAT/BAB – Bad Attitude, Bad Ability. This is the kind of employee who will take a miracle working middle manager to transform him or her into a force for good in the organization. A BAT/BAB is an employee who is in many ways irredeemable. This type of employee is the antithesis to the GAT/GAB. Their world-view is predicated on their belief that the glass is always half empty. They see problems where they do not exist, and can be a very undermining, undercurrent in the organization. They can poison the environment in the work place faster than an Iraqi Scud missile. They are employees who function at the lowest end of the performance scale. They are constantly trying to avoid work and shift tasks to others in the organization, all the while complaining about their intolerable workload.

When performance issues surface and are addressed with the BAT/BAB employee, the manager is showered with recriminations, excuses, and all manner of obfuscations. In light of the limited resource called time and the fact that miracle workers are few and far between, the best course of action with a convicted/committed BAT/BAB employee is to set a course for disciplinary action leading to termination. There is one word of caution about the BAT/BAB employee who has survived in any organization for any period of time. Employees like this have mastered the ability to disguise their true and essential nature. A discerning and wise manager must be willing to call a BAT/BAB a BAT/BAB and make a change, a change that will undoubtedly be for the better in the long run.

BAT/GAB, GAT/BAB – Bad Attitude/Good Ability, Good Attitude/ Bad Ability. The manager who works with these types of employees will inevitably expend huge amounts of time, discretion and discernment in understanding and managing them and their accompanying issues.

The hybrid mixture of ability and attitude that these employees exhibit will bedevil the most stable and resolute of middle managers. One minute when the good (attitude or ability) is in the ascendancy, the middle manager will want to celebrate that employee. The middle manager will literally be blown away with how adeptly they solved a problem or handled a volatile situation with a customer or fellow employee. The very next moment the middle managers hands will need to be pried off of the neck of that very same employee. The strangulation attempt will be the direct result of the employee irredeemably bollixing a situation or escalating a people problem beyond the middle manager's ability to repair. They have the inimitable ability to move from the polar extremes of good attitude/ability to bad attitude/ability all in the span of a single workday.

In an effort to reduce the exasperation coefficient for the middle managers left to manage this type of employee, it may be helpful to filter this employee through the context of the position that he/she occupies.

High Touch: Positions that have an abundance of interaction with customers and other employees is a high touch job. This is a job where customer service, communication, and human relations skills are of paramount importance.

The GAT/BAB employee may be an employee that the middle manager can salvage in a high touch position. It will be incumbent upon the middle manager to minimize the potential ability deficiencies of the employee while allowing the good attitude employee to bring their human relationship skills to the forefront.

In my own work experience I have worked with admission's people whose absolute strength was connecting with people and therefore maximizing the census and financial performance of the organization. However, many times these employees were poor processors of forms and producers of statistical reports. At one point in my career as a manager I made the judgment that one such employee's value in functioning in this high touch position far outweighed their failings in the details of generating forms and reports. I worked to structure the job to minimize the technical demands of the job and maximize the opportunities for this person to connect with the various publics that made our organization and that person successful.

By contrast, the BAT/GAB employee in a high touch position will serve as a constant source of frustration. Relationship problems between the BAT/GAB employee in a high touch position will be never ending and ultimately become unsolvable for the middle manager. To turn the above example upside down, imagine the same admission's position filled with an employee who was nuts on forms and reports but turned people off on a regular basis. The accountants would be happy with the forms performance but the organization would ultimately suffer due to empty units.

High Tech: Positions that require a great deal of technical knowledge and/or skill are high tech positions. This could include everything from computer programmer to a skilled machine operator. These jobs are absolutely dependent upon individuals with a pre-existing skill set, an ability to absorb and process technical information, or the ability to carry out defined, specific and exacting technical tasks.

The BAT/GAB employee, bad attitude and all, may be an employee that the middle manager may want to work with to make successful in a high tech position. The middle manager will have to attempt to design the job and work environment to minimize potential conflict between the BAT/GAB employee and other employees and customers. Additionally, they will need to play the role of peacemaker and negotiator when conflict inevitably arises.

To use an old world/old economy example from my own work experience, maintenance men are oftentimes BAT/GAB types. Good maintenance men have an abundance of skills and in very basic terms can fix stuff that breaks. They have a mixture of technical skills ranging from carpentry to plumbing to electrical to HVAC skills. A good maintenance man is invaluable in a 24/7, high use long-term care facility.

I have known many good maintenance men and have observed that sometimes they have personalities that do not lend themselves to positive human relations. They tend to like to work with things that don't talk. They can also tend to get into trouble when they start to interact with the unpredictable human beings that populate a nursing home.

In light of the fact that there is a finite and shrinking supply of people who have the broad and verifiable skill set necessary to be a competent maintenance man, my goal as a manager was to structure this position to minimize contact and potential conflict with other employees and customers. In spite of such efforts conflict would inevitably occur and when it did I reacted quickly and decisively to smooth ruffled feathers and resolve whatever situation had resulted. The goal was always to allow the organization to make use of the good abilities of this employee while trying to isolate the bad attitude.

The GAT/BAB employee, however, will not function well in a high tech position. I have known very affable maintenance people who had no skills with respect to the all-important technical side of their job. They could shmooze with the best of them but whenever they were confronted with a broken something or another, the GAT/BAB maintenance person would either stall for weeks or so screw things up that I would be forced to call in an outside technical person to undo the damage done by the well intentioned but incompetent GAT/BAB maintenance person. When the middle manager determines that they have a GAT/BAB employee in a high tech job they should understand that if they are not a miracle worker they should work with this employee to pursue options outside of the position that they currently occupy.

The attitude/ability paradigm outlined above is meant to serve as a tool for middle managers to help them wade through the endless streams of impressions and opinions (theirs and others) about employees that they are responsible for managing. Since these impressions can change from one minute to the next it is necessary for managers to have a means to categorize employees within the all-important context of the job that they are performing. This paradigm will allow the manager to determine which employees are destined to succeed (GAT/GAB), which ones should be removed from the organization (BAT/BAB), and which ones will require further analysis with respect to the type of position that they hold (GAT/BAB and BAT/GAB). This paradigm is intended only to lend structure to the thinking of the middle manager as he/she sifts through the emotionally laden pile of impressions and opinions about the human beings that they are responsible for. In the final analysis middle managers are not miracle workers. They can work with the employees on the margins. However, they cannot change the core essence of an employee nor can they resolve a basic mismatch between an employee and their position.

Feel Their Pain

The middle manager regardless of their socio-economic background will confront a multiplicity of backgrounds, home situations, educational levels, and economic stations that differ markedly from their own. The one certainty is that the middle manager will confront many points of disconnect between their own life situation and that of the employees that they manage. These points of disconnect will always be the case. The manager who uses Intuitment will acknowledge the fact that they cannot be all things to all people, but that they must seek to gain a greater understanding and appreciation for the lives that their employees have lived and are living while they are employed by the same organization.

The middle manager of the ones is faced with a diverse work force as well as one that is constrained in terms of supply. In the old days (the eighties) managers were always assured that if one employee did not work out there was a limitless supply of replacements lined up outside the front door eager and anxious to take the place of the employee who was a "misfit". In today's world the ready and abundant supply of labor is something that no manager can take for granted.

Because of this, managers must always be seeking to understand what their employees are confronting both on the job and in their life away from work. I worked with a manager who summarized this change in workplace dynamics this way. "In the old days if an employee was late for work you would pull their time card, make them come begging to your office at which point you would tell them they are gone. In today's world a middle manager will greet the tardy employee at the time clock, put their arm around the shoulder of the employee and seek to understand what is causing them to be late and if there is anything the manager or the organization can do to help."

Feeling an employee's pain necessitates a manager understanding what is going on in the life of the employee. This requires the middle manager to know their employees and to be connected to the workforce in ways that they can know what pre-existing job and life baggage an employee carries with them to the job or when an employee is facing problems in their current life.

This mindset hit home with me when I was pressed into manually writing checks due to a computer problem. For several pay periods I wrote out checks to employees and gained new insights into what my employees were living on. Subsequently when an employee who worked for me in rapid succession lost his car, his wife and was faced with riding a bike to work in an up state New York winter I was much more creative in helping this employee get past this crisis time.

Feeling an employee's pain is all about a middle manager acknowledging that points of disconnect exist between themselves and their employees and short of walking a mile in their shoes, need to actively and purposefully seek to gain insights into what their employees face in their daily battle to survive.

Feeling an employee's pain is not intended to be a free ticket to excuse bad behavior or performance problems on the part of the employee. A manager should seek to understand and when possible make accommodations for things that their employee is facing. However, at a certain point (that only the manager can determine) persistent performance problems or bad behavior cannot be excused by whatever an employee is facing in their life outside of work.

Make it Simple Silly (MISS)

The old adage about keeping it simple stupid (KISS) works in instances where the manager confronting a situation is the one solely and entirely responsible for framing the situation he or she is facing. Unfortunately in the real world, middle managers more often than not are confronted with situations that are interwoven with ancient history, high emotions, and well-established opinions. In cases such as this, the ability to KISS has spun out of the control of the middle manager by force of the multiple and confounding dynamics that operate inside of most organizations and that surround even the most simple of situations.

In instances where the situation has become hopelessly complicated by layer upon layer of history, emotions and opinions the middle manager needs to take a step back and Make It Simple Silly.

HISTORY: The middle manager must always be cognizant of the historical context and underpinnings of any situation that is confronted. The history can be personal or organizational. At times the history can be years in the making and cloud the vision of the manager as he/she attempts to clearly view the situation in a contemporaneous time frame. For example, when a manager is confronted with a situation involving a complaint from an employee who has been a chronic complainer for years, the middle manager will be tempted to ignore or discount the current complaint. The manager who is able to strip away the history of this employee and view the situation in its real time context will be much more able to act in a manner consistent with the present reality.

EMOTIONS: The middle manager must constantly strive to be aware of and neutralize his/her emotions when confronting situations. Emotions shroud the view of even the most stoic of managers. Emotions can revolve around the situation itself or the employee(s) or the department(s) involved. When the emotions of the middle manager or others are permitted to become part of a situation, it can take on a complexity and volatility that complicates resolution considerably. The manager who is able to recognize and control the emotional content of a situation will be able to see the situation much more clearly and divine a solution much more effectively.

OPINIONS: Opinions are cheap and everyone seems to have them. When a manager is attempting to assess a situation he/she should expect a plethora of opinions emanating from the lowest to the very highest echelons of the organization. More satisfying than Monday morning quarterbacking the areas favorite sport's team is the opportunity to second-guess the organization's response to a situation in the workplace. Since opinions are cheap and free speech a protected right in this country, the middle manager will be deluged with solicited as well as unsolicited opinions about what he/she would do in this particular situation. The higher up in the organization the source of the opinion, the more resonating that opinion becomes in the mind of the middle manager.

Cognizance and a studied determination to process and discard the majority of opinions about any situation will help the middle manager to see it more clearly. In the same vein, middle managers will be well advised to seek out and overlay the opinions of those with wisdom and insight onto any situation they face. By reducing the number of opinions that a middle manager allows to influence his thinking and the way he views a situation will help to make that situation simpler and cleaner to analyze.

Middle managers have at their disposal an abundance of strategies to make it simple. By making a situation simple, managers are able to reframe problems and remove the complicating factors that so cloud even the simplest of situations. With the problem stripped bare before them solutions can be seen in a clear, unfiltered light.

Internalize Listening

So much has been written about the need for all human beings to communicate better by learning to really listen. The manager who uses Intuitment will constantly strive to actively listen when analyzing situations. The key to internalized hearing is the active integration of what is said by an employee into the analysis of the situation the middle manager is confronting.

Internalized hearing is predicated on the middle manager taking the time to quietly hear what other employees involved in the situation are saying. A premium is placed on time and space that will allow for uninterrupted communication. This is not always easy to create in the hectic workplace. However, the middle manager who is able to intentionally communicate in this way will gain valuable insights and information upon which to base decisions.

The acid test of internalized hearing is imbedded in one key question for the middle manager. That question is, "have the words, thoughts, opinions and recommendations of the employee made enough of an impact that they have made it to the "OPTIONS TO CONSIDER LIST". The "OPTIONS TO CONSIDER LIST" is an actual concrete list of options that the manager will consider before he/she makes a decision. This list makes no guarantees about the fact that what any employee says will constitute the whole or any part of the decision ultimately made by the middle manager. However, the act of committing the thoughts, opinions, and recommendations of employees moves them from the vaporous realm of uncertainty to the concrete world of real decision-making. By reducing insights from employees to the written form the middle manager has moved from the certainty that what is said gets lost in the shuffling of the details to the possibility that what employees have provided by way of input can in fact have an impact on the analysis of a situation and the resulting decision.

Due Diligence

The next section of this chapter on situation analysis centers on the imperative that the middle manager take proper caution and pay close attention to details as they assemble the facts of a situation that is being investigated/analyzed. The importance of due diligence can be summed up in two basic concepts: *put it into writing* and *get it in writing*.

PUT IT INTO WRITING:

This concept of situation analysis places an emphasis on committing to writing the facts of the situation that is before the middle manager. Following the basics of "news reporting 101" the middle manager should strive to answer the basic questions of what, who, when, where and most importantly why. The middle manager will be tempted to fly by this important part of situation analysis as they hurry from one emergency to another. However, the "putting it into writing" part of situation analysis will not only enhance the clarity with which the manager sees the problem but provide a record for reconstruction when faces change and memories grow cloudy or selective or both.

WHAT: The middle manager should not overlook the importance of understanding and detailing what took place in the situation he/she is confronting. As was discussed earlier, oftentimes the presenting facts of a situation mask the real underlying situation. The "what" is factual in its presentation and includes as many details as possible. At this stage the manager should focus their efforts on obtaining the versions of those who had a first-hand, eyewitness connection to the situation. Until the situation is thoroughly understood the observations should not be deemed to be facts. As with all things in Intuitment, those who are in higher positions in the organization should not automatically be granted more credibility than those who occupy lower positions.

Finally, when recording the "what" of a situation the manager should seek to understand if there are precedents from previous occurrences that would dictate a certain response. This is critical because there is some innate part of an employee's memory that records all of the happenings of an organization. From the most minute and mundane to the earth shattering, employees will catch a manager applying different remedies to the same situation faster than the parking lot empties at quitting time.

WHO: The "who" includes not only the principles involved in the situation but those who witnessed first-hand what transpired. When determining who is involved in a situation, the middle manager must again make note of the obvious and dig deep to uncover those who may be operating in obscurity behind the scenes of any situation that is confronted. The middle manager should always seek to cross check names to assure that those who are involved according to one source were in fact involved. Identifying the "who" should include not only those directly involved in a situation but those who were witnesses to whatever the situation was. It is critical to have a clear idea of who was a witness and whether they were employees or individuals from outside the organization. For example, the implications of an employee argument in front of a prized customer versus a deliveryman who was in the wrong place at the wrong time may vary to a considerable degree.

WHEN: Time is not only fleeting but extremely elusive. People have a tendency to under or over report the time a situation lasted and may have very different recollections about when a situation occurred. The manager who is attempting to gather facts about a situation must be careful to conscientiously seek and report the times involved in situations.

WHERE: The location of an incident can have a material affect on how the middle manager responds to a situation. For example a heated argument between two employees in the break room or an office with the door closed will be handled differently than a similar situation put on display in front of customers in a very public location in the organization. Again, managers must be careful to accurately determine where the situation they are investigating actually occurred.

WHY: I can easily imagine my father saying something like, "It doesn't matter why it happened!" or alternatively, "It doesn't matter why you did it!". Middle managers do not reside in the black and white world of fathers. Since that is the case, managers must always be concerned with divining the "why" of a situation. The "why" of a situation will help immeasurably as the middle manager attempts to frame the context of the situation. By determining why an employee did something or why a situation occurred, the middle manager will gain greater clarity of insight and most critically allow for a more informed reaction to the situation as well as more lasting and long term solutions.

Learning why an employee did something or why something occurred is not prospecting for excuses. I believe that managers sometimes overlook the "why" of a situation because it seems to be a sign of weakness or signals a willingness to accept excuses. Quite to the contrary, the "why" of a situation helps the manager understand how to prevent the situation from occurring in the future. It also allows the manager to adjust any disciplinary action that might spill out of the situation. For example, an employee who just had his wife leave him the evening before will not excuse an angry tirade. However, it may make a difference in what step in the disciplinary process the manager takes as a response (along with past work record, where the exchange took place, with whom the exchange took place, etc.).

GET IT IN WRITING:

When a manager is analyzing a situation many facts will fly in his direction. Much will be superfluous and non-essential. However, there will be key bits of information from employees and others that will be essential to the investigation of the situation. When these essential pieces of information become apparent the middle manager must acknowledge an immutable law of human nature. This law holds that as time passes and as pressure increases, people's memories become very hazy and unreliable. The middle manager who reacts to a situation on the basis of information he has received from others that gets lost in the passage of time and convenient lapses of memory will be dammed to failure.

"Get it in writing" simply means that the middle manager will take due diligence in getting key pieces of information from others in writing. Once this is done the middle manager has the individual affix their signature to their statement. This invariably does two things. Primarily it protects the middle manager from a person's story being altered in the future. Secondarily it tends to weed out information that may be of questionable accuracy or veracity. It takes a measure of commitment for someone to put something into writing and then to sign it.

Don't Sweat The No-Brainers

The rainbow-like profusion of situations that middle managers confront is rich in texture and endless in variety. These situations range from inconsequential to life/career changing and everything in between. The shear volume of situations that a manager needs to analyze can quickly overwhelm the resources available to him/her.

Middle managers who make use of Intuitment have a construct at their disposal for reducing the number of situations that require careful consideration and analysis. Intuitment holds that managers should sift situations that are before them and quickly and surgically cull from the universe of situations the "no brainers".

"No brainers" are situations that have an absolute certainty imbedded within them with respect to the need for actions as well as the action that needs to be taken. "No brainers" are situations that common sense and universality of opinion would dictate the need for, and type of, action to be taken.

In my life as a middle manager I have confronted many such situations. One of them stands out in my mind as this chapter is being written under a swelter of 90% humidity and 90 degree temperatures. It was one such day when my maintenance person came to me and indicated that a compressor in a roof top air conditioning unit had gone bad. He was beside himself with anxiety because of the expense in calling someone out on a Friday late afternoon to make the necessary repairs. Even though this was the absolute appropriate and only response he was concerned about the effect that this service call would have on his budget. By the time we spoke he was worked into a twisted frenzy of apprehension and doubt.

We had no choice. If we put off this repair the health and possibly the lives of our residents would be put into jeopardy. It was truly a "no brainer". We arranged for the repairs and the residents spent a their weekend in air-conditioned comfort.

By failing to recognize this situation as a "no brainer" my maintenance person frittered away valuable and limited time and emotion. This was time and energy that could have been focused on analyzing other situations that would have benefited from thoughtful, careful situation analysis.

When a middle manager sees a "no brainer" he/she should do as the situation indicates and then move on to analyzing other situations that are more in need of deliberation and consideration.

Summary

Situation analysis is foundational for every response a manager takes when confronted with a situation in the work place. The failure to do a comprehensive and thoughtful job of situation analysis will doom the response of the middle manager to any and every situation.

The survival of every middle manager is inextricably linked to their ability to carry out thoughtful and thorough analysis of situations that the workplace gives birth to on a regular and recurring basis. By carefully walking around situations the middle manager will improve the likelihood that their response will be reasonable and insightful and ultimately judged to be the correct and appropriate response.

Chapter Ten

Situation Response

Situation response focuses on the context of the manager's response to a situation. The context of the manager's response to a situation is concerned with strategies, attitudes and values that frame the response. In many ways the way that a manager responds to a situation will equal or exceed the importance of the response itself.

The survival of the middle manager is predicated on many things both real and imagined. One of the definitive determiners of a manager's survival is how they respond to situations. Employees below and mucky mucks above are always watching and evaluating how managers respond to situations. The following SAV's will help middle managers maximize their opportunities to respond to situations in ways that build and affirm their performance as middle managers.

Always, Always Respond

The manager has limits to what he controls on a daily basis. So much of what he does in response to a situation is prescribed by organizational realities, policies, and procedures. As a result the manager is often times cast in the role of messenger. He or she is the one who delivers the pronouncements and judgments from on high that arise from a particular situation. The more centralized and bureaucratic an organization the more the manager is simply the communications link between the organization and those that are managed. In spite of this reality the manager is always in control of the follow-up for every situation that they confront or that is brought to their attention.

When confronting a situation, managers must focus on and accentuate what they can control. What they can control is the simple yet character-defining act of always responding to a situation. The path of least resistance is always the path that we as human beings wish to follow. For managers this means ignoring situations because they would be too much trouble to deal with or forgetting (conveniently or otherwise) about following up on a situation that has been brought to their attention or that they have stumbled upon. Inaction is always easier and less filled with conflict and the uneasiness that stalks the path of every manager.

A manager's main, and sometimes only, stock in trade with the employees that they manage is their credibility. This credibility is an elusive thing but is in many ways it is built upon the manager's dedication and attention to following up on situations. Employees are very perceptive. They can see quite clearly when a manager is no more than a puppet with the strings being pulled by a whole host of mucky mucks. They have probably seen this their entire working lives and I think for most employees have come to accept it as a fact of life in corporate America. What they cannot tolerate is a manager who is so disorganized or frightened by conflict that they fail to follow up on situations. Managers with a desire to survive must never fail to follow up on any situation.

Unrelated but closely connected to responding to situations is responding to questions or queries from employees. Managers get pulled in many directions and do not relish the role of being the answer guy who always is the bearer of bad news. Managers are the recipients of many questions and queries from employees over the course of their workday. Some are rhetorical, some are genuine and some are simply meant to make the manager squirm. Regardless of the motivation, managers need to always respond to questions that originate from employees. Again, regardless of the content of the answer the simple act of following through will confer legitimacy on the manager as manager and take away a very damming characterization option for employees. A manager who is characterized as, "*Don't bother asking him/ her, they never get back to you*", will have lost a major portion of the leverage that is needed to balance this very difficult middle management equation.

Timing Is Everything

As with the proceeding section, managers are not always afforded the luxury of establishing their own time line for responding to a situation.

However, when a manager is in the position of unilaterally establishing a time frame for responding to a situation, they should take care in determining when to respond. Since establishing an ideal time for responding to a situation is so dependent upon the situation, and situations are so widely variable, I will focus on the two extremes of the response time continuum: responding to a situation too quickly and alternatively responding too slowly.

Too Quickly: There are many problems with responding to a situation too quickly. First and foremost situations are almost always laden with an emotional content. Managers as well as employees involved in a situation may experience a range of emotions. When these emotions are negative they can poison a situation involving even the most professional and controlled of individuals. In this context managers should always seek to avoid responding to a situation too quickly when emotions (theirs as well as others) are most likely to come into play and have a deleterious effect on decisions made and reactions that flow from those decisions. In my experience as a middle manager time has always had the effect of ameliorating the emotional content of any situation. The elimination or diminution of the emotions surrounding a situation will always increase objectivity and the effectiveness of the manager who is able to separate the situation and any decision made concerning that situation by the simple passage of time.

Managers who respond too quickly to a situation will negatively affect their ability to see the entire situation. Time is an indispensable ingredient in allowing a situation to be brought into the full light of objective and critical analysis. When a manager responds too quickly, due diligence will not be possible with any degree of thoroughness. The quality of a decision will inevitably reflect this fact.

Finally, managers who respond too quickly to a situation will take away the possibility of a solution materializing out of the ashes of the same situation. On many occasions I have been struck by the fact that the resolution to a situation was imbedded in the very core of the matter at hand. By allowing time to pass, the manager is able to see if there is an ideal solution that is buried within the situation itself. By rushing to a response the manager does not allow for this possibility to materialize.

Managers who respond too quickly to a situation may sate their emotional need to "do something". Their superiors may view such a manager as decisive and proactive. Such managers may be able to get things off of their "to do list" more quickly than other managers. Unfortunately in the long run they may make decisions that will fail to serve the organization, its employees and in the in the final analysis themselves.

Too Slowly: Procrastination is something that is part and parcel of the human condition. Managers not unlike anyone else are tempted to put off the usual unpleasantness of responding to situations. Waiting too long to respond to a situation creates several potential difficulties for the middle manager.

First and foremost the longer a manager waits to respond to a situation the more likely it is that inertia will set in. As a manager gains distance from a situation it becomes easier with each passing day to simply "let it go". At times this will be a conscious decision because in retrospect the situation does not merit a response.

However, there are other times when the path of least resistance is to simply let the situation fade from the memory and recede into the forgotten past of the organization and the manager. As times passes from a situation the manager will by force of human nature be less and less likely to respond. This is not a good development for the middle manager as will be discussed below.

Situations that involve employees and that revolve around performance issues or behavioral problems have a defined window for the manager to rectify the situation in an optimal fashion. In this window of time the manager has to first convince the employee that they have done something wrong and then teach them the proper/correct way to do their job or conduct themselves.

As time passes from a situation the manager will be less and less likely to take full advantage of this "teaching point". Likewise employees will more than likely convince themselves that they did nothing wrong or someone else or something else was really at fault. In our age of instant victimhood and relative humanism, everyone seems to have a free ticket to do and think whatever they like and stand in judgment by no man. Managers need to avoid waiting too long to respond to a situation so that this teaching opportunity (fleeting and illusive as it might be) does not pass away, never to be recovered again. By responding in a timely fashion the manager maximizes their ability to teach the employee while at the same time maximizing the receptivity of the employee involved.

Waiting too long to respond to a situation opens the manager to a wide variety of potential accusations and problems. With the passage of time memories grow cloudier with each passing moment. A manager who waits too long to respond to a situation will likely be confronted by all manner of denial, obfuscation and backpedaling by those involved. "I didn't say that", "I didn't mean that", "That's not what I saw", etc. will flow from the lips of those around the situation. Managers must balance the need to do a righteous and proper job of due diligence with the fact that the passage of time is no friend of their efforts to discern the truth.

Managers who wait too long to respond to a situation will invariably open themselves up to charges that they are being arbitrary concerning what they choose to respond to. An employee who is involved in a situation and does not hear anything for days and days will rightfully believe that the matter is concluded. When the manager descends upon them one fine day with some sort of disciplinary action they will justifiably ask why. This employee will believe that the manager is incompetent, arbitrary or engaging in harassment. Managers must be ever vigilant against waiting too long to respond to a situation and thereby creating a perception that they are being capricious in how they deal with situations and employees.

There is no magic formula for determining the proper timing of a response to a situation confronting a middle manager. Managers must always seek to balance the tendency to react too quickly with the natural disposition to drag their feet. This balance can only be struck with a good awareness of the inherent problems with the outer and inner limits of the response time continuum.

ID The Button Pushers

Every human being has certain issues, buttons if you will, that evoke a strong emotional response. Managers being human have similar buttons that when pushed by other people have the potential to push him/her over the "edge". Sons, daughters, and spouses usually have great insight into the buttons that will send their parent or spouse into orbit. Likewise in the workplace certain employees have an uncanny ability to know what issues will push a manager over the edge of sanity and reason.

Intuitment places a premium on a manager knowing him/her own self. This knowledge is far ranging and covers a number of factors of a manager's make-up. At the top of the list is an awareness of what issues, subjects or situations have the potential to turn even the most staid and stoic of managers into a tongue lolling, crazed lunatic. A manager who is armed with this knowledge and insight will help in avoiding and dealing with close encounters with button pushers.

Hot buttons come in all shapes and sizes. They can be as simple as an employee who has a penchant for beginning every question of a manager with the rejoinder, "*I am sure you will have to check with your boss before you can answer my question, but…*". Hot buttons can be as complex as a passive aggressive employee who is in a position with time critical expectations and an uncanny ability to stall and obstruct every project that is placed on their plate.

Whatever the hot button issues are, the middle manager must avoid the all too easy expedient of expressing with cavalier abandon something like, "*I am not the last bit bothered by that employee who, (fill in the blank with whatever hot button issue is being discussed)*". It is human nature for all of us to discount the effect that others have over us. Whenever I verbalize that someone or something does not bother me it always means that that someone or something bugs the snot out of me. Usually the more that I say that I am not bothered, the more likely I will be to have a mental meltdown the next time I am confronted with that same person or situation.

Once a manager has honestly assessed what their hot buttons are, they need to identify the people and situations in the organization that will cause them to respond in a less than desirable fashion. Once a manager has identified these issues that make them crazy and the people and situations that will bring these issues bubbling to the surface they can take steps to avoid or diffuse potentially volatile and damaging situations. The failure to identify hot button issues and button pushers will place the manager in the position of making mistakes in responding to situations; mistakes which are wholly avoidable by simple introspection, analysis and anticipation.

Actively Manage WOP – T and WOP – S

Managers live their work lives in a fish bowl. Managers are the fish and everyone else in the organization stands around on the outside watching the managers do what they do, namely manage. Employees observe everything that the manager does and says. Interest in what the manager does is most keen when he/she is responding to a situation. Such occasions generate a level of interest akin to Super Bowl Sunday.

Most managers realize the fact that they are under the microscope and being watched by the mucky mucks as well as by peers and those that they manage. For some managers this fact can create a vague sense of unease. For others it can manifest itself in panic attacks as they get in the car to drive to work. For all managers it is imperative that they make a conscious and concerted effort to manage their response to what other people in the organization think and say about them.

The active management of WOP – T (what other people think) and WOP – S (what other people say) begins with the simple yet momentous act of acknowledging that what people say and think about us DOES matter. The overwhelming majority of people care what others think and say about them. A similar number can be heard mumbling, "I don't give a crap what he says (thinks) about me!". There is an old adage that he who excuses himself, accuses himself. In a similar way those that trumpet the fact that they do not care about what others think/say about them are by the simple act of vocalizing this fact announcing that at a core level they DO care. It is human nature to care about what others think/say about us and is reinforced by our society's obsession with the way we are seen in the eyes of others.

Managers making use of Intuitment will acknowledge that they are in fact affected by what others in the organization think and say about them. Once they have taken this all important first step and acknowledged this fact they will set out to develop a means to actively control the deleterious effects of being consumed with the thoughts and words of others. The act of controlling the thoughts that can invade every quarter of a person's consciousness will take time and effort.

Besides causing uncontrollable facial twitches the tendency to be concerned with the thoughts and words of others can have a direct and deleterious effect on the quality of a manager's response to situations. Facial twitches are bad (I have experienced them) but allowing those who are not in a position to have legitimate input into a response is by a far measure worse. Yanked this way and that way by what someone might think or say about a manager's decision will result in vacillation, impotence and eventually a totally ineffectual manager.

The manager who can recognize the potential negative effects of WOP - T and WOP – S, can develop means to control being overly concerned and sensitive to the thoughts and words of others inside of the organization. Managers who are so freed will be able to respond to situations independent of the shackles of these phantom and very real thoughts and words and as a result will render more objective and effective responses to situations.

Return Serve

When I was trained as a manager I was told that there is no more inviting trap for an ill-mannered employee to fall into than presenting a problem or concern to the manager. Traditional management theory held that whenever a manager is confronted with a problem or concern voiced by an employee, the simple retort, "Well what do you suggest as a solution to that problem", would forever rid the manager of the need to deal with that problem ever again. It was called getting the monkey off of the manager's back and sending him screeching back onto the shoulders of the unsuspecting employee. I almost felt that whenever this occurred I should rub my hands together with glee and mock the employee with a jubilant, "Nah, nah, hah, nah!".

Intuitment posits that whenever an employee presents a problem or concern the manager should use it as an opportunity to begin an honest back and forth dialogue. The goal with return serve is for the middle manager and employee to jointly seek a solution or an answer that will benefit the employee, the organization and the middle manager. Building upon the synergy of ideas described in the previous chapter, employees potentially represent a very fertile source of creativity and solutions to situations if properly cultivated. Unfortunately the old world approach of scornfully throwing a problem or concern into the face of the unsuspecting employee halts this dialogue before it is ever started and cuts off this valuable resource for the middle manager.

Managers who return serve should take on the role of initiating follow up conversations and contacts with the employee whom they have asked to help them solve a problem or address a concern. The manager should do this in a very non-threatening manner and openly share any preliminary observations or ideas that they may have come up with on their own. The process may or may not result in a solution but the cultural norm that problem solving is a joint exercise will be established and reinforced over time.

Golden Rule, Common Sense

There are several universal laws that managers should observe as they respond to situations. They rely heavily on common sense and the golden rule.

Utter The Unutterable: Managers oftentimes suffer from the misconception that after they have assumed the mantle of middle manager that they in some mystical way receive as part of the package the gift of infallibility. This misconception is due to several factors. First and foremost middle managers are always aware of the giant scorecard that is kept by the mucky mucks that rule the corporate kingdom. Managers perceive (correctly in many cases) that when a magical number of mistakes or failures is noted on the scorecard, their time with their employer will be drawing to a close. With this world view it is in every manager's best interest to hold the number of mistakes and failures to a minimum. The other reason for managers to deny and hide mistakes is the sense that they have to put on a front of infallibility with the employees that they manage. It is widely accepted that a manager's credibility is directly linked to his/her ability to minimize the number and severity of mistakes that their employees become aware of.

Taken together these forces create an environment that is ripe for managers to deny that they have ever made a mistake, even when they have. Unfortunately for the employees who work for these, "pictures of perfection" they are seldom afforded the satisfaction of a manager saying to them, "I was wrong." or "I made a mistake."

Managers who have internalized Intuitment have come to accept their own fallibility. When such a manager makes a mistake that has a direct and negative impact on an employee they never hesitate to tell the aggrieved employee that they were wrong. By doing this simple thing the manager has taken away an all too easy reason for the employee to harbor malice toward the manager or the organization or to fail to care about their job/the organization, etc. The manager by admitting a mistake has also allowed the employee to cast off feelings of powerlessness, negativity, cynicism and inferiority (basically the feeling that they are the only one in the organization who makes mistakes and regularly has them shoved down their throats).

The power of admitting an error to an employee cannot be understated. I once had a boss who over the course of years that we had worked together only once ever admitted that he had made a mistake. It was an earth shaking confession on his part until he attached to his, "I was wrong...", the totally deflating suffix, "...to have trusted you.". My feelings of outrage and defeat were equal and overwhelming. Suffice it to say that any admission of being wrong on the part of any manager should never include their employee's shortcomings or failings. An admission of failure on the part of the manager to an employee should be unconditional. More damage is probably done with a conditioned acknowledgement of error than simple silence.

Closely connected to the admission of an error is the act of expressing sorrow. The simple yet earthshaking expression of, "I am sorry." Directed at an employee is as hard to deliver as the previous, "I am wrong." It is difficult for managers to utter these words for many of the same reasons and invariably place the manager in a vulnerable position.

However, a simple and sincere "I am sorry." can communicate empathy and a connection to that employee more profound than any other utterance that a manager could possibly make.

It is difficult ever to say that you were wrong or that you are sorry. Human nature rebels against such admissions and expressions. In point of fact one's personal life as well as work life these expressions are the salve that heals the wounds begotten by our all too human failings. Middle managers who are able to judiciously and appropriately express their humanness through words of sorrow and admissions of failings will create an enduring bond with their employees greater possibly than any other thing they could ever do.

Equal Time: Managers who respond to situations ultimately end up discussing the situation with the employees involved. This discussion is oftentimes done within the context of a disciplinary action. At times such as these, managers are oftentimes so consumed with the situation or the discomfort of the meeting that the message tends to be heavily weighted toward hard cold facts and the negative aspects of the situation. The reality is that human beings have a natural distaste for negative messages about themselves. We all tend to become defensive and obstinate when confronted with information that runs counter to our idealized notions of our self as well as things that we are involved in. This oftentimes results in a disconnect between the manager and the employee whose behavior he/she is trying to modify. When a manager confronts an employee with negative information about their performance and they shut him/her down the potential for positive change drops to zero.

For this exact reason Intuitment places a premium on managers always seeking to balance positive and negative feedback when communicating with their employees. When a manager is aware and able to mix the message (positive things about an employee and their performance as well as negatives about their performance) the employee is infinitely more receptive to criticism and more energized to change behavior.

Use Boogeyman with Discretion: The world of the middle manager can be filled with thoughts and realities that bespeak an unsearchable impotence. This impotence is part and parcel of being stuck in the demilitarized zone between those who wield power in the corporate world and the employees who make the corporate cyborg operate on a daily basis.

With so much time spent in a position of relative powerlessness the middle manager can feel like he is marooned on an island with his group of mutiny prone employees. The middle manager is alone to cajole, manage and in some way move his/her employees to do the bidding of the organization. With such a daunting task the middle manager is often tempted to resurrect the omni convenient boogeyman. Managers typically do this when they are in the position of representing some sort of aversive position or taking some unpopular action with the employees that he is responsible for. The manager will begin his pronouncement with the immortal words, "*The Boss*" or "*The Board*" or "*The Corporate Office*" wanted me to do "so and so" or "such and such".

Employees really do know the score relative to the power equation inside of an organization. They are big people and usually have figured out that managers have limits as to what they can, and cannot, do. They do not view this as an inherent weakness of the middle manager, but rather a fact of corporate life. However, when a manager plays the corporate boogeyman card too often employees are left to feel that the manager is not only powerless but in some respects clueless and possibly cowardly. Cowardly in the respect that the manager is unable or unwilling to do the "heavy lifting" of unpleasant news. Managers should not fall into the habit of blaming those on the top of the organization for everything bad or unpleasant that needs to be communicated to employees.

What Goes Around Comes Around: Whenever I was getting dumped on when I was growing up my mom would always say, "Don't you worry Kevin, what goes around comes around." Her meaning was quite simple.

Whatever bully or nasty teacher was giving me a tough road to hoe would eventually get "theirs". Her hidden meaning was that my oppressor was destined to meet an unfortunate end to their miserable life.

I have come to believe that there is a positive side to this old adage. Namely, acts of kindness and goodness shown to others would be rewarded if not in this life then in the next.

Managers should always be aware of this adage as they carry out their sacred trust of managing other human beings. No matter how powerless a middle manager might feel he/she always has more power than those he manages. With this power comes a responsibility to treat others with dignity and respect. Failing this I believe that managers will come to the same fate. I have seen it in my own life and believe that justice is eventually served.

On the other side of this adage-equation, managers who treat their position as a trust and act toward their employees with respect and dignity will reap a transcendent loyalty and respect from them. While this may not translate into corporate success it will yield a harvest of respect and goodwill among those that are managed.

Minimize Use of Messengers: Managers should distinguish themselves by their willingness to get their hands "dirty". Literally in the sense that managers should have no compunction about jumping in and doing the dirty work and jobs of their business or industry. Likewise a manager should have an identity as an individual who is willing to carry bad news to employees in person.

Managers have an unprecedented number and variety of "messengers" at their disposal for communicating bad news to employees. These include everything form E-mail to V-mail to memos to the always popular subordinate. What is common to all of these messengers is that they represent the path of least resistance. These messengers allow an easy means for the manager to extricate himself from the hot seat reserved for the bearer of bad tidings. These messengers are for the most part impersonal and safe for the middle manager in the short term. In the long term this is another story.

Managers should be willing to confront an employee, or employees, face to face and communicate the distasteful stuff that is part and parcel of life in an organization. Employees may not like the message (e.g. your employment is being terminated) but they will for the most part appreciate the courage required and respect shown by dealing with the employee directly and as an adult.

Chapter Eleven

A Look Back, A Look Forward

A Thankless Job

If I had a quarter for every time that someone told me, "Kevin, I wouldn't have your job for anything." or some variation on this lamentation I wouldn't have to continue my hand-to-mouth middle management existence. I am of the firm belief that middle management is the quintessential thankless job.

Middle managers spend the majority of their existence between a rock and a hard place, between the devil and the deep blue sea, or my personal favorite between a paperweight and an oak desktop. Managers are caught between employees with discernible skills that inextricably link them to revenue generation. They suffer under the heavy thumbs of superiors who many times lack patience for the long term and exhibit the petulance of a sleep and food deprived toddler. In addition, middle managers are in the unenviable position of holding a position that everyone in the organization believes that they can do better than the middle manager currently holding the position.

In many respects middle managers are often in the position of doing their job at the pleasure of the employees that they manage. The odds very much favor employees when arrayed against the numerically small and insignificant (in terms of direct connection to revenue generation) middle manager. This is borne out most convincingly when perusing the employment classified advertisements. The clear demand is for employees with discernible and discreet technical skills. Most employees have figured out the equation that says one middle manager does not equal the sum of the employees that they manage. Sensing this basic inequality, employees can quickly understand that they have an inherent advantage when dealing with middle managers. The middle manager must strike a balance between outright capitulation and using the full extent of the authority that is available to him/her. This equation changes from day to day, situation to situation, and employee to employee. Therein lies the challenge and the inherent thanklessness of dealing with the employee side of the management equation.

Dealing with those above the level of the middle manager is no less fraught with uncertainty and danger. Mucky mucks have the power to control the very life and death (hopefully only in the career sense of these words) of the middle manager. This power is vested in them by the organization and can be absolute and totally arbitrary. Laws and corporate sentiment do not favor the person who holds the position that can be most easily second-guessed in the entire organization. Everything from what have you done for me lately to the bottom line to the subjective grayness that envelopes everything that the middle manager touches makes his/her value to the organization a totally ephemeral reality.

Finally middle management is a thankless undertaking because there is an almost universally held belief that any non-manager can magically be transformed into a manager and that any career manager is a dime a dozen commodity.

There is a common belief that a non-manager can be magically and instantaneously transformed into a manager by simply bestowing upon him/her a hocus pocus blessing and providing him/her with the sacred three-volume set of policies/procedures, laws/regulations, and management 101 textbooks. Anyone who has survived any time at all as a middle manager can attest to the absolute absurdity of the notion of sacred books and mystical blessings. Managers are neither hatched nor magically extruded from a mold of incantations and the three pillars of traditional management theory. Managers grow into the profession over time and through trials that cannot be replaced by the artificiality of passive learning in a cloistered academic or corporate environment.

The other universally held belief that discounts the value of middle managers is that managers are a "dime a dozen". Quite possibly because they tend to be generalists (at times hewing to the old adage, "mediocre in all, proficient in none.") this misconception continues to exist. It is as if the corporate world readily envisions dozens of wide eyed, fresh faced manager wannabees lined up outside the HR door ready, willing and able to replace a middle manager who has outlived his/her usefulness.

Taken together these two perceptions cause most managers to question their own value. Likewise those who ultimately control the destiny of middle managers have devalued them to the point that they have become a commodity, replaced at their very whim.

A win/win situation is the Holy Grail for middle managers. Unfortunately most of the situations that managers deal with are pre-ordained to torque off one half of the equation or the other (bosses, employees, customers). With our increasingly vindictive, polarized and contentious society, middle managers very seldom make everyone happy. The job of the middle manager is carried out in a battle zone. The manager is left in the unenviable position of attempting to broker a peace between warring factions, at times bent on each other's mutual destruction.

All of this makes the thankless job of middle manager all the more thankless and hopeless for those of us who toil in the trenches of middle management.

"Failure" Pre-Ordained

Throughout my twenty years as a middle manager I have experienced innumerable positive things. Likewise I have also come to know intimately the reality of and never ending nature of "failure" (failure is in quotes because they were failures only in the sense of the corporate judgment accruing to my sin of commission or omission). I have experienced both big and small "failures". I have also witnessed my "failures" blooming into the ultimate ignominy of involuntary termination. "Failure" is an integral part of the life of a middle manager. It is the ultimate reason for a manager to realize the impossibility of their task, the paucity of the tools available to them and the need to maintain a detached, objective sense of self worth and competence.

There are two problems with the concept of "failure" as it relates to middle managers. The first problem is the fact that "failure" is purely a subjective concept. Sure there may be obvious, universally embraced instances of failure such as the Enron collapse, but these are the exception. The overwhelming reality is that "failure" is not a matter of black and white but rather an amalgamation of colors that produce a most stark and distinctive shade of gray. In my personal experience so many of my "failures" were the result of spin doctoring by those above me and subject to all sorts of outside pressures and circumstances. The pressures and unrelated circumstances as well as the uncontrollable factors that shroud all that a manager does make "failure" a fait accompli.

The second major problem with the reality of "failure" in the global sense of the concept is that there is no universal scoring system for "failure". Not only is there no universal scoring system, but there is no way for managers to know where they stand in terms of their performance vis-à-vis their "failures". A manager does not get an earned run average or a quarterback rating to know how they stack up against others on any objective scale. A middle manager for the most part lives day-to-day with the knowledge that pre-emptive termination is real and present, and a fact of life.

Since "failure" is pretty much unavoidable, middle managers must be realistic about this reality. This includes learning from "failures" and maintaining an objective and realistic view of "failure". To take "failure" personally and believe that it in some way diminishes the inherent worth and value of the middle manager is to sentence oneself to a whip lash existence of highs and lows, with the lows inevitably swamping the psyche of the middle manager.

What Tools?

Much of this survival guide has focused on debunking the notion that the three traditional tools available to managers are equal to the task that confronts them. This well-established and universally embraced belief has done great damage to the profession of management as well as a total disservice to many a middle manager.

First and foremost this belief has created a perception on the part of the public and those in the corporate hierarchy that management is a defined science that has a predictable flow from problem to resolution to happy-ever-after ending for everyone involved. Further, it is widely held that anyone with the proper training and resources can master this simplistic cookbook approach to management.

In addition, this belief has planted a seed that has grown into a mighty oak tree protruding squarely from the cranium of most middle managers. This oak tree is best represented as a feeling of inferiority and incompetence whenever the situation at hand is not amenable to correction by rote application of one, or all three, of the pillars. When failure inevitably and invariably occurs managers are left with an empty feeling that can undermine even the most resolute and thick skinned.

As a result, managers are left to feel like losers while the rest of the universe shakes their collective head in disbelief. The three traditional tools of management are simply tools that provide structure to a manager's actions. They are no guarantee of success nor do they insulate the manager from "failure'. Any manager who has experienced the inadequacy of the three traditional management tools has sensed the need for something more.

Intuitment - An Aide to Survival

That "something more" is a concept that I have dubbed Intuitment. It is a mindset and an approach that offers only one guarantee. Intuitment's one and only guarantee is that the manager who practices what it teaches will experience a freedom and a release from the conventions that have made the practice of management a game with an abundance of victims littering the corporate landscape.

As has been said earlier, Intuitment is NOT a panacea or a guidebook to answers to unanswerable questions and problems. Just as the manager's search for answers very seldom reaches an unequivocal solution, so too Intuitment is not a distiller of absolute truth.

Intuitment will not change the inherent thankless nature of the middle manager's job. However, it will provide ways for the middle manager to deal more effectively with the employees they manage and the bosses who control their daily destiny.

Intuitment provides a number of strategies, attitudes and values for bringing balance to the equation with employees on one side of the inequality sign and managers on the other. These SAV's are straightforward and not magical by a far stretch. What these SAV's do is provide managers with ways to get employees slowly but surely on their side. The goal for the middle manager is to bring his/her employees around to the thinking that the success of the employees, organization and middle manager are inextricably linked. This is far from an easy task. Yet the SAV's that are imbedded in Intuitment will give the middle manager the best chance of mastering the conundrum that is employee relations.

Likewise Intuitment provides SAV's for grappling with the omnipotence that the mucky mucks enjoy over their middle management chattel. These SAV's are aimed mainly at allowing the middle manager to gain freedom from the fetters that can choke off the self-image and self worth that is so tenuously held by most middle managers, for the majority of the time.

Finally Intuitment provides a strong argument against the belief that middle managers can be created out of thin air at very discounted prices. Intuitment holds that a manager's skills are built slowly and deliberately over time. The skills that a manager amasses are the product of experiences of both a positive and a negative nature. These experiences cannot be distilled into a book of policies or of lofty ideas. They must be lived out in the crucible that is called middle management.

Failure is inevitable. Failure, whether it is universally acknowledged or simply the by-product of spin administered by a cowardly/backstabbing boss will always be a reality that middle managers will need to deal with. Intuitment provides a means to place failure in perspective and allow managers to frame it in a context that allows for growth and minimizes the potential for damage to the confidence and psyche of the middle manager. Just as bosses can spin anything into a clear example of failure so middle managers need to objectively evaluate situations with bad outcomes in the light of growing through the experience of bad things. Intuitment holds sacred the concept that failure should always be something within the control of the middle manager that is being labeled as such.

A Final Word:

This guide for middle managers is intended to make the difficult, if not impossible, task of the middle manager a more survivable experience. Survival only and most importantly in the sense that the middle manager maintains a world-view that places the entire management odyssey in the proper perspective. That perspective holds to the essential and unalterable fact that management is 10 parts art and one part science.

Managers who use this survival guide and all that Intuitment teaches will continue to experience failure. They will continue to toil in a thankless job. They will work in what is on many days, and in many respects, a no-win situation.

However, they will also understand the bankrupt notion that the three traditional tools available to managers are somehow sufficient for the task at hand. They will also analyze situations with new insights, respond to situations differently, and in general view their world from a fresh perspective. A perspective of hope about what can be accomplished with the judicious application of common sense, the golden rule and this tool called Intuitment.

EPILOGUE

As the final work on Middle Management Survival Guide is being completed I find myself going through a situation that hauntingly echoes the words of this book. As a middle manager I have found myself in a situation where the facility that I am "running" has run into financial difficulties borne of a core change in our local marketplace. This change has resulted in a precipitous drop in census and as one might imagine, revenue.

The second guessers have materialized out of nowhere and are currently circling overhead. I am pressed in on all sides and the specter of involuntary termination is moving ever closer. My body will soon join those that litter the corporate landscape of the ones. It is simply a matter of time.

However, until the final pronouncement is delivered and my execution assured I will continue to use the advice that this book contains. I will continue to carry out my responsibilities as I have done for the past twenty years. I will not surrender, but continue to fight the good fight. I will move to another position with my self-concept and psyche unbent and unbroken by the forces that assail me along with every other middle manager.

Thank you for reading this book and considering all that it contains.